Relationships
in
Recovery

Relationships in Recovery

A Guide for Sex Addicts Who Are Starting Over

Linda Hatch, PhD

Pentacle, Santa Barbara 93103
© 2013 by Linda Hatch
All Rights Reserved
First Printing: June 2013

ISBN: 978-0615820071

Interior Design: Benjamin Swihart
Cover photo of Shadows on Grass by
Pierre Des Varre, Zurich, Switzerland

Table of Contents

Foreword

Deeply rooted within the experience of finding, growing and maintaining intimate relationships, whether romantic or platonic, is the emotional meaning that truly makes our lives worthwhile. So it makes absolute sense that when the days grow short, and the time we have left on earth can be counted in days, rather than months or years, few of us wish we had spent more time working or making money, yet nearly all of us long for more precious moments spent with those we have loved. This is the human condition.

For most sex and love addicts, despite our common histories of disconnection and non-intimacy, the process of recovery often brings with it a renewed and healthy desire to bond. Yet unlike those whose backgrounds and early life experiences have left them with an innate capacity to make this happen, most recovering sex addicts have little to no idea how to go about the process evolving intimate, honest connections to other people. Among the many losses resulting from a lifetime spent in active sex and love addiction is that past patterns of relating to sexual and romantic partners were more often more about control, emotional escape and disconnection, than genuine attachment and emotional meaning. As a result, even in recovery, our long-term relationships can lack depth and true meaning.

And this is where this long-needed book, *Relationships in Recovery*, written by my esteemed colleague Dr. Linda

Hatch, comes in. *Relationships in Recovery* provides the full gamut of information required for recovering sex and love addicts to either turn an existing relationship into a healthier, more fulfilling connection, or to develop new relationships that have life and meaning beyond the superficial. Yes, there have been an unending number of previous books written about the process of finding, developing, and maintaining healthy intimacy, but in reality the vast majority of these are practically useless for those in sexual addiction recovery, as our initial starting point is often so very different than that of most other people. And no, one addiction is not just like another addition in this arena, as many other types of addicts (drug addicts, alcoholics, shopaholics, compulsive gamblers, and the like) typically start out with a healthier understanding of relationship development than do those of us for whom *"out of control"* sex and intimacy were the problem in the first place.

Happily, Dr. Hatch recognizes this fact and begins *Relationships in Recovery* at the "sex addict's starting point," by helping the reader identify the ways in which one has historically selected partners and related (or not related) to them. Essentially, for sex addicts to develop trustworthy intimacy, they must first identify and acknowledge the dysfunctional patterns that have in the past kept them at arms' length from meaningful connection. Only after the past has been evaluated, integrated and moved beyond, can workable intimacy, dating and relationship goals be achieved.

This book rewards the reader with clear structure toward evolving relationship boundary plans similar to those utilized by sex addicts when first learning to define their sexual sobriety. As this is already a familiar process to many in recovery, it ends up being a user-friendly and wise methodology. What I particularly like about this book is

the deep insight it offers into the many relationship road-
blocks experienced by sex and love addicts—not only
when active in their addiction, but also after having
achieved meaningful sobriety. These problem areas are
particularly well delineated in Chapter Nine, "Using Basic
Recovery Skills to Deal with Ten Common Relationship
Challenges." And it is worth noting here that I often see
these very issues repeatedly presenting in my own clients.

One man in particular, Steven, comes to mind. Both during
his active addiction and over the course of several years in
recovery Steven had made numerous attempts at relationships. However, at the first hint of the other person being
less than perfect he would immediately decide that the relationship wasn't going to work out because the other person
had "too many shortcomings." From then on he would behave in ways that sabotaged the relationship, oftentimes
pushing his partner's buttons in ways that made the partner
seem even less "right" for him. I worked with Steven on
this core behavioral issue for quite some time until he began to understand how he had been making mountains out
of molehills, thereby leaving his relationships doomed to
fail but also avoiding what was for him, a frightening scenario, one of being vulnerable to true intimacy.

The guidance *Relationships in Recovery* offers to recovering addicts like Steven is, in my opinion, very much on
point. In fact, it is quite similar to the advice I gave to
Steven: *Use the same tools that kept you sexually sober
toward finding relationship health.* And it is amazing
how well this works! Over time Steven learned to accept
others as they were, and to not constantly take their inventory. He stopped searching for faults in his partners and
began to look for their shared values and interests. Thus,
over time, he was able to evolve the very kind of healthy

relationship he had always sought out, but had been unable to maintain.

At the end of the day, our basic human needs for attention, validation, and intimacy are healthy and universal. We all need to feel loved and appreciated and have a sense of belonging. Unfortunately, sex addicts repeatedly abuse the experience of romance and sex, seeking shortcuts around the vulnerability required to form deep and lasting bonds. Engaging in the illusion of intimacy by having anonymous sex, abusing porn for hours or even days at a time, having repeated affairs and/or regularly using prostitutes—can feel powerfully fulfilling in the moment and provide a brief simulation of intimacy, but, over time, these shortcuts often deliver more emotional emptiness than fulfilling nourishment. Thus, for many sex addicts the process of finding and embarking upon a healthy, non-objectified monogamous relationship is more than just a luxury, it is a necessary and vital part of lasting recovery. In the pages that follow, Dr. Hatch offers recovering sex addicts the vital direction and information needed toward creating the kinds of connections that bring the kind of meaning and fulfillment we all want, but don't always have the skills to create.

Robert Weiss, LCSW, CSAT-S, co-author of *Closer Together/Further Apart: The Effect of Technology and the Internet on Sex, Intimacy and Relationships*, is an addiction therapist, educator and internationally known expert in the treatment of sexual addiction and intimacy disorders. Dr. Weiss has also served as a media specialist for CNN and *The Today Show*. A blogger for *Psychology Today*, he currently serves as Senior Vice President of Clinical Development for Elements Behavioral Health.

Preface

The premise of this book is that although romantic relationships can be problematic for anyone, they are particularly problematic for recovering addicts in general and for recovering sex addicts in particular. Special problems arise for sex addicts in that sexual addiction is conceived by those who experience it, no less than those who treat it, as an intimacy disability. I have attempted to describe the nuts and bolts of how and why this disability creates particular challenges for sex addicts in recovery seeking a relationship, and to set out what I hope will be some helpful guidelines for overcoming them.

Although addressed to sex addicts, I believe that most of the program that is set forth will be entirely applicable to other kinds of recovering addicts who have experienced relationship problems while they were active in their addiction. For any addict, the past problems with intimate relating do not necessarily disappear with the advent of sobriety.

This book is addressed primarily to those who have achieved sobriety and are interested in finding a new partner, or repairing a relationship that predated their recovery. I believe that the latter, repairing an old relationship in recovery, is a process identical to starting a new relationship; hence, I treat it as identical for the purposes of this book. While I may discuss such issues as dating and choosing partners, I intend for this content to be applicable quite literally to addicts who are working on a relationship with their prior spouse or partner.

This book may also be of interest to spouses and partners of recovering sex addicts or to people who are dating recovering sex addicts. However, it is not intended as a recovering couple's guide. In addition, I have not attempted to deal extensively with most of the broader issues in the area of healthy relationships, since there are many other excellent books and programs relating to those more general relationship issues.

I believe that sex addicts, and those with other addictions as well, need to be in fairly stable recovery (through addiction treatment, counseling, 12-step program work or ideally a combination of these) before they are ready to be in a romantic relationship. Furthermore, I believe that a relationship in recovery has a much better chance of succeeding if the recovering addict goes on to gain the additional level of self-awareness and does the kind of preparatory work described in this book. Sobriety is a necessary prerequisite, but it is only the beginning. As the saying goes, "Recovery takes a lifetime."

I. Introduction: Learning a New Relationship Style

Imagine living without the fear of loving and not being loved. You are no longer afraid to be rejected, and you don't have the need to be accepted. You can say 'I love you' with no shame or justification. You can walk in the world with your heart completely open, and not be afraid to be hurt.

Don Miguel Ruiz, *The Four Agreements*

Addictions and Relationships

In general, all addictions can be said to be relational. They have to do with relationships in their origin, in the way their symptoms are exhibited and in the nature of the treatments that alleviate them. That there is a disturbance in the area of relating is more evident in the case of sex addiction than in most other addictions. In sex addiction the addictive behavior is usually a form of relating that is separate from the rest of the addict's life. No matter what the sexually addictive behavior is—whether it is serial affairs, anonymous sex, online hook-ups, prostitutes, pornography and even masturbation to fantasy—it is a compartmentalized and secret part of the addict's life that has to do with a compulsive, sexualized relationship to another person or to a representation of another person.

Relationships with significant others in the sex addict's life are compromised due to the sexually addictive behavior. The sex addict is addicted to something which threatens his or her bond to a partner in an obvious way. And once the addict's partner has found out about the addiction, they most often see it as a form of betrayal. Other addictions such as gambling, drinking and compulsive spending also adversely affect intimate relationships, but the behavior itself appears to be unrelated to the close relationships. The spouse of an alcoholic or compulsive gambler may feel lied to, ignored or devalued. They may even feel that their partner is behaving in a passive-aggressive or vindictive way, but they can still see their partner as loyal to them. They do not necessarily feel they are being cheated on as a spouse or partner.

So all addictive behaviors have the potential to seriously compromise an intimate relationship and all are symptoms of impairment in the addict's ability to relate intimately to other people. For some addicts this impairment extends to other kinds of relationships as well. They feel self-conscious, uncomfortable or inferior in relation to people they work with or people they interact with socially. Other addicts, including many sex addicts, seem to interact quite comfortably with friends and associates; people trust them and like them. And yet even when this is the case, sex addicts may feel somehow fraudulent. They know on some level that they have not integrated the separate parts of their lives and, in fact, something is missing from these seemingly normal friendships. That thing is the ability to fully and honestly invest themselves in the relating.

Being split off in the way that sex addicts are allows their addiction to progress to greater extremes of behavior and greater levels of compulsiveness for a long time without being discovered. Compared to a person in a later stage of alcohol or drug dependence, the sex addict may seem less deteriorated. It is known among sex addiction therapists that sex addicts whom we encounter in treatment are likely to be in much worse shape than they seem to be on the surface. It just doesn't show in their physical and cognitive function in as obvious a way. So the challenges for recovery are the same but different. The alcoholic may believe, erroneously, that once he or she is sober, intimate relationships will take care of themselves. The sex addict may feel the same way but, more often than not, the recovering sex addict has great difficulty envisioning a committed intimate relationship and a healthy sex life with a partner.

It is the good fortune of recovering sex addicts, as opposed to other kinds of addicts in recovery, that they are more aware that their addiction has implications for their relationship life. Sex Addicts Anonymous, and most sex addiction treatment programs, suggest that the addict have a sober dating plan before starting to look for a new relationship, and that they should also engage in a couples' recovery program and a couples' 12-step program such as Recovering Couples Anonymous as basic to rebuilding the trust in their existing relationship. There is a general acknowledgement that they may lack some basic intimacy skills and relationship skills, and that they should get counseling. But the process of learning and practicing this new model of intimate relating is more complex and challenging than many people realize.

Approaching Relationships in Recovery

The same relationship problems that exist in recovery existed prior to the sex addict becoming sexually sober.

Even at best, a practicing sex addict has relationships that are likely to be intimacy-disabled in some way. These patterns are old habits, and the addict in recovery will bring them with him or her in the new attempt to form a bond. Below is a simple self-test to illustrate the indicators of relationship problems that typically occur in addiction. They are not specific to sex addicts, but they give a general idea of the things experienced by people with impaired intimacy and relationship abilities.

Addictive Relationships Self-Test

1. Growing up I didn't see my parents as consistently loving, and contented with each other.

2. My relationships typically start with an intense sexual attraction and rapid involvement.

3. I find it easy to start relationships, but they always get complicated.

4. I find it hard to know how to get out of a bad relationship.

5. I sometimes think I stay in a relationship because I am afraid of being on my own.

6. I am afraid of my partner's anger.

7. I sometimes placate or manipulate my partner to avoid confronting things.

8. I find it easy to get into thinking that my partner is to blame.

9. My partner and I don't talk about our feelings about the relationship.

10. In my relationships one person is always less devoted than the other.

11. Either I feel superior to my partner, or I feel my partner is superior to me.

12. I am dishonest with my partner at times to avoid upsetting him/her.

13. When I am in a relationship, my partner and I don't socialize with friends as a couple very much.

14. Either I or my partner is always trying to get us into some kind of therapy.

15. I feel that having a good relationship is hopeless.

When you look at this list of statements, it should be clear that what I am calling addictive relationships are characterized by things like negativity, turmoil and alienation. In other words addictive relationships are dysfunctional because they lead to feeling bad, afraid or in conflict much of the time. An intimate partnership should be a good experience, not a bad one.

All of the above items indicate the potential for deeper problems, problems that sex addicts typically bring with them as they emerge from their addiction. These problems are not limited to addicts alone, but they tend to reflect the *core negative beliefs* addicts have about themselves, which in turn draw on those early attachment problems that are the common antecedents of sexual addiction. We will go into more detail regarding early childhood issues in Chapter V. These attachment issues and negative beliefs, although mitigated in recovery, are likely to emerge in subtle ways as the recovering addict attempts to venture forth into the realm of intimate relating.

Addictive Relationships and Core Negative Beliefs

Addicts typically have a history of relationships that demonstrate and support their *core negative beliefs*—beliefs about their own lack of self-worth, their lack of faith in others and their need to hide who they really are. Thus their "intimate" relating tends to be characterized by dishonesty, judging, blaming, fear of abandonment and conflict.

- *The lack of feelings of self-worth* will express itself alternately in feeling better than and/or feeling worse than their partner.

- *The person who is afraid to be honest* and is ashamed of their feelings will be isolated, and their relating may take the form of a "zero sum game," i.e., "If I win you lose" and vice versa.

- *The insecurity and shame* may manifest in a competitive "victimized" style and a lack of empathy.

- *The inability to believe that other people can help* meet their needs can result in their being manipulative or in their becoming a "closed system," being "needless."

- *The core belief that they are unlovable* will lead to the need to do things for the partner, to do everything right in order to be approved of and loved, leading inevitably to resentment.

One of the most important signs of healthier relating will be the ability to see oneself as equal to others—no better, no worse.

A person who is so-called "intimacy-abled" can form a healthy *intimate* **and** *sexual* attachment with a partner in adulthood. This implies the ability to trust your partner, to trust your own ability to set boundaries, to communicate your feelings, to be able to commit and to relate to a partner with all aspects of yourself, and not to lead part of your life in shame and secrecy, separate from the one you love.

Are you ready for a relationship?

No one is perfectly ready to start (or reconstruct) a relationship in recovery. Your individual recovery will be a lifelong process of internal growth. No matter how solid your recovery from your addictive acting out is, you may approach the idea of dating or finding a new love with much trepidation. You are not the same person as you were before recovery, and now you will be confronting a potential partner with a new you. Nothing will be pre-programmed; none of your old routines will be appropriate. And yet what is most likely to happen is that you will experience a *"first relationship out of the gate"* syndrome in which you find yourself doing a lot of things differently, and yet you end up repeating some of the old behaviors.

Depending on your old patterns of addictive relating, you may find yourself attracted to someone who is going to cause you problems. I have heard a woman in recovery talk about a new relationship "becoming addictive," meaning that she was feeling some of the old sexually addictive feelings in relation to the new person. These old addictive feelings could involve hyperarousal and fantasy, obsession with the person or the relationship, fear of intimacy, secrecy, reemergence of trauma reactions and so on.

On the other hand, you may feel a lot of apprehension about relationships and tend too much to avoid pursuing anything with someone. In starting over with relationships there are so many different ways to fall into something that is not right that it would probably be a miracle if anyone got it right on the first try, although I'm sure it has happened.

It might help to think about some of the progress you have made in the areas that contribute most to your ability to find, and hopefully keep, a good relationship. These are some of the characteristics that would tend to support your readiness to try again:

1. I am more aware of what I am feeling at any given time and I am more able to identify feelings and think and talk about them.

2. I have taken care of my basic health needs including having an STD test and other routine tests. If I have been prescribed psychotropic or other medication, I follow up on appointments and on the use of medication.

3. My ability to focus on whatever I am doing is improved, and I don't feel anxious and pulled in different directions as much.

4. I enjoy having "down time," and I don't feel like I have to do something all the time.

5. I have learned that I can go to a counselor or other person I trust for help or advice, and I can listen to what they say even if I disagree.

6. I am aware of any problems I have with other addictions, and I have done what I needed to do to address them.

7. I have found ways to keep myself accountable regarding my addiction that rely on people other than a spouse or partner.

8. I am willing to try out new activities and interests and I am OK if some things I try don't work for me and others do.

9. I am willing to experiment with changing my daily ritual.

10. I have a greater sense of what I want and need and am clearer on what things interest me in life.

11. I am more interested and confident in my work or other activities.

12. I am more flexible and more tolerant than I used to be.

13. I feel like I can stick up for myself when I need to without going overboard.

14. I am not as self-conscious about initiating a social contact, and I can be more comfortable just being myself.

15. I no longer feel anxious or apprehensive when I am alone. I would like a partner, but I am OK without a partner.

Compulsive Deprivation and Relationship Readiness

Although out-of-control behavioral compulsions always contain some element of their opposite, over-control and self-deprivation, there are some sex addicts who are far more weighted in the direction of over-control. These addicts feel threatened by the idea of relationships and tend to be rather isolated or have very casual contacts. They do not feel deserving and are uncomfortable with closeness.

They tend to deprive themselves in various ways including sexual anorexia, lack of self-care, underearning, and living a minimal lifestyle.

Once you as a recovering addict have identified your own deprivation side, you will have looked at ways to overcome these fears and practiced both getting comfortable with giving yourself and trying new social behaviors. You do not have to be perfect. As you will see from the following chapters, most of the ideas and exercises can also apply to those addicts whose relationship problems also include residual tendencies toward avoidance and deprivation. As with all addicts, good relationships will not just happen to you out of nowhere. You will have to think about change on a basic level.

I usually encourage people to try dating as soon as they feel they are in solid sobriety (usually around a year) and feel they are ready to venture forth. The process of trying to relate intimately to another person can be a great way to understand yourself better and to enhance your growth in recovery.

Are you ready to resume a preexisting relationship?

For the most part, I believe that sex addicts in recovery cannot go back into a preexisting marriage or partnership just because they have been in recovery for a period of time. At some point addicts need to give themselves time to examine their relationship patterns and partner choices. I think it takes time apart from a partner to do this. Some addicts think about this in terms of "dating" your old spouse or partner and really starting over from scratch. I think the important point here is that part of being ready to reenter a relationship is realizing that *things can never go*

back to the way they were. And being willing to look at why.

Later we will deal more with relationships as a learning experience and with relationships as a form of spiritual practice. I do not suggest that you follow a rigid set of rules about when to resume or start attempts at a relationship. You will have to judge for yourself. If it is a mistake, you will learn from that too.

What is a "Relationship Style?"

I am defining a relationship style as composed of the following:

1. The overall tone and rhythms that characterize the relationship,

2. A configuration or set of roles that addicts and their partners play with one another, and

3. An underlying set of attitudes or beliefs about the function of relationships in one's life.

For sex addicts the style in which a relationship is carried out is determined by many of the same early experiences as the addiction itself and also serves to support or perpetuate the addict's sexual acting out behavior.

I see the term 'relationship style' as similar to the term 'arousal template.' Arousal template is used to describe the particular set of stimuli (images, events, circumstances), based on early experiences which lead to sexual arousal and orgasm and which are repeated compulsively in addiction. The addict's relationship history usually reveals a set pattern or configuration that is less than optimal and is intertwined with the addict's sexual arousal template.

I have chosen the term relationship *style* instead of relationship *template* in order to avoid confusion between patterns of intimate relating and patterns of addictive arousal although, as we will see, the two are parallel in many ways.

Changing Your Relationship Style

The set of tools in the following chapters is intended for all people dealing with relationships in recovery whether they are in a relationship or are looking for one. The concepts and tasks in the chapters below are applicable to:

- Addicts with relationships which have survived disclosure and sex addiction recovery and want to start over with the same person to forge a healthy marriage or committed relationship.

- Single people looking to date and find a partner with whom they can have a healthy, intimate and fulfilling relationship.

The tasks are the same because even for a committed couple in recovery, the intimacy and relationship skills are simply not there. *The partners in a married couple will need to learn to relate in a totally different way, and they will be starting a new relationship from scratch. Any other way to think of it is based on illusion.* Without this basic level of change, people carry their addictive patterns into the future and thus limit the level of success they can hope for in close or romantic relating. Relying on their old ways of relating, the couple will be able to share only part of who they are with their partners and continue to be cut off in one or more ways. In a worst case scenario, these old patterns may lead the addict back into sexually addictive, unhealthy and dangerous behaviors.

But addicts in recovery may not have a clear idea of exactly what they were doing in their love relationships that made them so problematic. You can't change what you are not aware of, so much of this book deals with becoming more aware of what you have been doing in your relationship life and why. And even if you have gained a much greater level of awareness about relationships through your recovery so far, you may not have tried out that awareness in real life behavior. It may take some practice.

The following chapters will offer some definitions and central ideas relating to intimate relationships, and a set of tools and tasks aimed at helping people learn new ways of thinking and behaving in relationships and overcoming the old fears and patterns of relating.

Although integrating sexual intimacy into a love relationship is part of the process, the emphasis here will be on the more basic assumptions and priorities. In order to integrate healthy sex into a relationship, the partners have to first have a healthy foundation to their relating. I hope that what follows will help you to better understand the key characteristics of your addictive relationship style and provide a series of tasks to help you change that relationship style to one that promotes commitment, contentment and growth.

Laying a Foundation—Work on Yourself First

Although the tools and tasks described below may be used by couples, they are not intended as a couples' workbook. The work of taking your recovery to the next level, of becoming ready for a healthy relationship is *individual work first and couples work later.* So although partners or would-be partners may benefit from discussing their work with each other and sharing ideas, the work itself is internal to each partner. It consists of building a foundation upon which each addict or partner of an addict can hope to build a healthy, intimate relationship. As you think about starting over in relationships, you should be aware that taking this step may be challenging and stressful, and at times you may feel discouraged. It may even constitute a sobriety challenge, and this means that you will need to rely on the fellowship that you have established in your recovery and your trusted advisors to help you along the way.

II. From Addictive to Healthy Relationships: Identifying Your Old Relationship Style

Man is involved in karma when he interferes with the world in such a way that he is compelled to go on interfering, when the solution of a problem creates still more problems to be solved, when the control of one thing creates the need to control several others.

Alan Watts, *The Way of Zen*

The first step in changing your relationship style is identifying those patterns that characterized your relationships (or lack of them) before you began your recovery journey—*your old relationship style.* Some addicts will find that they can identify one or more different relationship styles that they have had in their life as an addict.

As you will notice in the examples of addicts' relationship styles given below, relationships are not all bad, but they tend to be characterized by negativity, stress or unpleasant emotions on and off much of the time. This negativity can take many forms such as feeling long-suffering, feeling inadequate, feeling intense abandonment fear, bouts of anger, nagging guilt, agonizing jealousy, or loneliness. In this sense your old relationship style as an addict was just one more manifestation of your addictive thinking and your negative core beliefs about yourself. *Looked at this way, your pattern of relating in your addiction is a form of acting out behavior, acting out of experiences from childhood.*

Some styles of relating actually *are* the acting out of an addiction and others are almost the opposite of the acting out behavior. But in any case there is bound to be a connection between the way the addict functions as an addict and as a partner. There will be more about the origins of relationship dysfunction and the laying down of these patterns in Chapter V.

If you are familiar with the writing of Patrick Carnes, you will notice that there exists in each of these relationship descriptions the basis for a relationship acting out cycle similar to the sexual acting out cycle described by Dr. Carnes. Whereas the sexual acting out proceeds from ritual to acting out to shame to despair to fantasy and back to ritual, the relationship cycle begins with distancing (through conflict or withdrawal) and proceeds to resentment, shame or blame to avoidance of intimacy and back to distancing.

Sexual Addiction Acting Out Cycle

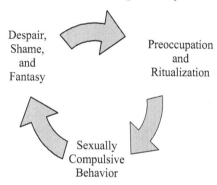

Despair, Shame, and Fantasy

Preoccupation and Ritualization

Sexually Compulsive Behavior

Addictive Relationship Cycle

Avoidance of Intimacy and Resentment

Conflict and Withdrawal

Shame and Blame

Below are some of the common types of relationships that addicts engage in along with a description of how that style might *support* the addiction. In later chapters you will look at your relationship history and your relationship progression over time to look for changes, patterns and attempts to "get it right." Hopefully, the relationship styles described here will stimulate your thinking about your own relationship history.

Examples of Addictive Relationship Styles

The High Drama Style

High Drama relationships substitute intensity for intimacy. They may begin with a powerful sexual charge and are characterized by confrontation, conflict, mistrust and power struggles. Fear and strong emotions fuel the instability and therefore the intensity. It is typical of such relationships that there is always some form of "triangulation," meaning that the intensity is kept going by the fear and threat of a potential romantic triangle. The extreme mistrust and lack of openness lead to a relationship that is fundamentally one of *competition rather than cooperation.* Finding subtle ways to hurt, undermine or guilt-trip the other person alternate with overt conflict and betrayal. If there is any stability, it tends to be a kind of détente, where each person holds something over the other. One or both partners have accepted the idea that the overpowering emotional intensity of their relationship is a sign that it is the right relationship, the most significant relationship they will ever have. They may justify their chaotic situation by thinking that "normal" happy, contented relationships are unimaginative, boring and undesirable.

How the High Drama Style Supports the Addiction

The High Drama relationship can *be* the acting out, or part of it, i.e. the partners may be engaging in sexually compulsive, objectifying or risky behaviors with one another, although their relationship is devoid of any healthy intimacy. Or the addict (and sometimes the partner as well) may be engaging in their own separate sexually compulsive behavior outside the relationship, in which case the drama of the relationship creates a chaos that either justifies or covers up the outside addictive behavior. Sometimes the partners have created a situation in which they know or suspect each other's sexually separate life, and the drama is part of the ritual of mutual intrigue, suspicion and betrayal. This creates a vicious circle of resentment, conflict, retaliation, blame, shame and more acting out.

The Separate Life Style

These relationships lack drama and seem to be characterized by harmony and cooperation. However, in such relationships the basis of what seems to be a "working partnership" is one of avoidance and alienation. Most frequently the addict partner is acting out sexually outside the relationship and the other partner is *"checked out,"* leading his or her separate life while basically choosing to ignore any red flags that suggest the other person is leading a double life in the sexual realm. The addict's underlying belief is that he or she cannot have their sexual needs met in a close relationship. The partner's underlying belief is that if they try to relate more intimately and explore what is really going on, they will be abandoned (or harmed). They feel, therefore, the only safe relationship is an alienated one. The lack of a fuller bond tends to make both partners feel devalued, and the result is a deadening stagnation.

This style of relating may be present in a lot of relationships in which the addict and their partner have a "public persona" as a couple in which they are seen as highly functional and desirable. They may present the picture of an ideal family, participating in all the appropriate community activities and behaving in ways that are seen as socially responsible and exemplary. It is assumed by others that because they look good superficially that they therefore have a good marriage or relationship, when in fact they have the shell of one.

How the Separate Life Style Supports the Addiction

These relationships do not attempt to be more than a partnership, and the overriding goal is to keep the peace. This means that the addict has arranged the relationship so that there is literally neither a requirement for, nor an expectation of, intimacy and he or she is safe in leading a secret life involving sexually compulsive behavior, safe from discovery by the partner. Sometimes the lack of sexual intimacy, or even of attraction, in the relationship is a justification for the secret sex life. In any case there exists a situation that is unfulfilling but in balance. There is diminished chance that the addict will be found out, or that there will be consequences for the sexual acting out behavior, unless and until it becomes so extreme that it can no longer be ignored. Thus the couple may go on this way for a long time.

This style sometimes necessitates the addict play a public role of stability and strength which very likely is experienced by him or her as an act that they must play. The feelings of deceptiveness and phoniness add to the addict's overall level of shame and low self-worth and thus further fuel his or her need to act out sexually in order to get relief.

The Rollercoaster Style

Some relationships have elements of both the High Drama style and the alienated "separate lives" style. Intensity, suspicion and confrontation alternate with avoidance, secrecy and manipulation. This pattern bears some resemblance to the so-called *abuse cycle* in which there is a repeated pattern of a build-up of tension and mistrust culminating in a blowup that is then followed by remorse and a "honeymoon" period.

These couples are sometimes convinced that they have a happy marriage or relationship, and that the only problem is *the one little issue* relating to the addict's sexual acting out. The addict may abstain from sexual acting out for periods of time only to be caught in a betrayal or a lie that signals a relapse. This in turn causes drama and conflict attacks and counterattacks and sometimes visits to the therapist's office.

How the Rollercoaster Style
Supports the Addiction

When the dust settles, nothing has really changed despite the best intentions of both partners. What the partners are missing is that the "one little issue" is not little at all. Rather it is indicative of a lack of intimacy and relationship skills in the relationship *as a whole*. The addict is able to continue to hold on to the addiction and avoid the need to really face the underlying problems by finding ways to convince the partner that he or she is really "trying" or by using "treatments" or "therapies" that are somehow guaranteed to be ineffective or abandoned. The "co-addict" in this situation believes that it is possible to get the addict to change and believes it each time promises are made. Neither partner is willing to take a stand and take the risk of losing the relationship, and he or she instead settles for a status quo. Although there are many variations on this theme, one common pattern is to perpetuate this unsatisfactory situation because both partners are in a sense in denial. They are both avoiding the shame of confronting something which they feel shows them to be inadequate. This in turn fuels the disappointment, dissatisfaction and resentment in both partners which in turn feeds the pattern of betrayal, suspicion and conflict even more.

The Hostage Style

This is a relationship built on the premise that one of the people is "broken," and the partner takes it upon him- or herself to "fix" them. This is a relationship that is common in other addict codependent situations such as alcoholics and their partners and resembles a parent-child relationship. There is no opportunity for genuine intimacy since the relationship is predicated on inequality: One person is "OK," and the other person is not. *The relationship is built on a perceived need rather than mutuality and respect. This means that the relationship is one of a broad category of relationships based on unequal power.*

The partner in the parent, doctor, or rescuer role has usually picked someone who needs "fixing" because it is a way to feel safe from ever being abandoned. The "patient" or "child" partner consciously or unconsciously accepts this role because they are not required to be responsible and emotionally mature. Also they are pretty sure that the parent figure will remain loyal as long as they stay needy, because the parent figure needs to be needed. *Many sex addicts play this "broken" role in their relationships long before their sexual acting out ever comes to light.*

If the more powerful figure is the addict, then this style can play into their arousal template of needing some kind of dominance or control in relationships and their partner then enters into the sexual acting out of that addictive scenario. Regardless of who plays which role, Hostage-style relationships can easily slip into High Drama or Rollercoaster-style relationships.

Sometimes there is a genuine "feeling" of caring and closeness in relationships built on dependency. This may take the form of a parent-child nurturance or fondness. But if one person has significantly more power or re-sources, and the other person is dependent on them, then they cannot leave the relationship without incurring dire consequences. They are in a way held hostage. They also cannot "disobey" the powerful partner, as they have given up control of their life. They are OK as long as they keep their partner happy.

How the Hostage Style Supports the Addiction

When the dependent partner is the addict, the expectation that he or she is incompetent, impaired or irresponsible in some way allows the addict to be deficient in relationship skills and in interpersonal skills generally. They are in a situation in which their intimacy disability is accepted and seen as part of their identity. If they are sexually acting out it may be overlooked or minimized for a long time and so they are not required to do anything to get help. The addict may resent their one-down position, but they are willing to make the tradeoff and act out sexually for release. The addict's immature moodiness and impulsivity are likewise minimized since they reinforce the partner's role as caregiver. This is a relationship style that can go on for a long time before the addict's underlying resentment causes his or her addictive behavior to escalate to a degree that it is finally addressed.

If the addict is the powerful or parental figure, then the addict gets to set up a relationship to suit his sexual addiction. Although it is an arrangement that supports the addiction, it is an inherently unstable basis for a relationship and is usually temporary.

The On Again-Off Again Style

This is a familiar pattern among addicts and partners of addicts. Addicts and their partners seem to particularly suffer from a kind of acute and chronic "approach-avoidance" conflict. They never get beyond a certain point in a relationship without a rift and a separation. By the same token they never really end the relationship. The addict will swear that this time the relationship is *really* over. He's had it! But the next thing you hear he will have texted his "ex" or she will have emailed him. If he breaks down and contacts her it is because he "wants to make sure she's doing OK" (whatever that means). If she emails him on business, he begins reading into the contact and imagining that she wants to get back together, or wants to see him, or wants to have sex with him. (All of this may be true on some level.) In this situation the relationship itself is a form of mutually codependent behavior that is based in fear and an inability to take responsibility for directing one's own life.

How the On Again-Off Again Style Supports the Addiction

The fact that this type of on-and-off relationship is in no way a real relationship with a future (or a past!) means that the addict stays more or less stuck in a situation that offers no alternative to his or her addiction and no motivation to change. The addict can stay isolated with no real relationship and yet convince himself that he has a relationship. This pattern is one that particularly suits the addict who is also subject to compulsive self-deprivation. In this case the sex addiction and the deprivation addiction feed on one another. The deprivation compulsion means that the addict will be either outright unable to connect with anyone or will be in severe conflict about it. The isolation and lack of ability to feed himself emotionally or any other way means that the addict continues to feel underprivileged and over-entitled to sexual acting out, and it also means that he can continue to feel that he must wait for someone or something outside himself to make things better.

The Un-Relationship Style

Many sex addicts have a series of partial or truncated relationships, finding themselves unable to move past a certain point in forming a bond. These may be the "seduction role" type of sex addict addicted to repeated sexual conquest without commitment as described by Dr.

Patrick Carnes (1991), or they may simply find they cannot move into another level of intimacy or connection even when their sexual compulsion has nothing to do with actual people, e.g. pornography addicts. Some recovering sex addicts crave an intimate and sexual relationship with a real person but never get past the level of fantasizing about people. They spend time around strangers or casual acquaintances hanging around coffee shops, taking classes etc. but they find it impossible to actually connect with someone they are attracted to. Their attempt at bonding and intimacy could be called an Un-Relationship. Other types of "un-relationships" are those experienced by people who habitually have sexual chat room, phone, or web contact with people they don't know or don't ever meet. These behaviors, like all forms of acting out, tend to escalate over time.

How the Un-Relationship Style Supports the Addiction

Obviously, not having relationships at all tends to make the way clearer for the addict's sexual acting out behavior, whatever that is. No one is there to spy on him or her, or to suspect or confront him or her. The addict has created a lifestyle built around the lack of intimate romantic relationships and can easily use this lack as a reason why they need to engage in the acting out behavior, e.g. pornography addiction, phone sex, prostitutes, even sexual offending behaviors. One of the beliefs of such addicts that I have heard over and over is some variation on, "If I only had a beautiful woman (or the right man) to love me then I wouldn't need to be a sex addict." This one sentence clearly shows how the deck is stacked; there is no thought of what the addict needs to do to *be more loveable*, only that he wants someone to come along and love him. We will return to this issue in Chapter VIII.

Examples from Real Life (no real names used)

Bill and Joan

Bill and Joan were an outwardly happy couple for many years. Bill's sexual addiction—voyeurism and fantasy about much younger women and seductiveness toward women outside the marriage who were in a dependent role to him—was never discovered or addressed during the marriage. Bill was a successful professional, and the couple had plenty of money. Joan was flirtatious with men outside the marriage and also liked to look at other men. Both Bill and Joan were very jealous of one another. They came into conflict often, usually about jealousy relating to sexuality. Although they were frequently creating sexual triangles or attempting to discover each others' imagined betrayal, they were in a kind of uneasy détente most of the time. They gave as good as they got. Both partners were dishonest and devious. When Joan did something behind Bill's back, there were confrontations. When Bill did something that got Joan upset, he placated her with expensive gifts.

The relationship between Bill and Joan was sexually charged, and both of them liked the fantasy of a three-way with another participant. They were both interested in watching pornography, especially with a three-way theme. Although apparently sexually suited to one another, their relationship was emotionally impoverished due to their conflicts and their lack of honesty.

By the time I saw Bill for sex addiction treatment, he was already married to someone else, someone very unlike Joan. The new partner initiated therapy because she could not tolerate Bill's roving eyes, interest in much younger women and inappropriate and objectifying comments about women. She hated sexual intrigue and hated the idea of pornography or three-ways. Bill was eager to be in therapy, as he felt that his new wife was his soul mate, and he would do anything to make things right in their relationship. In therapy Bill has been able to understand much of what was wrong in his first marriage as part of his recovery and his awareness in general.

Bill and Joan's Relationship Style

This relationship has elements of both the High Drama and the Hostage style. The relationship was sexually charged with a constant undercurrent of drama due to the mutual suspicion, betrayal and intrigue and therefore fits the Drama style. The conflict and drama led to alienation and distance, while the level of dishonesty between them made genuine closeness impossible. The element of the Hostage style comes in due to the unequal power relationship. Bill made the money, and Joan was being placated with expensive gifts. Joan was materialistic and liked the gifts and it never occurred to Bill to actually deal with whatever he had done to upset Joan. He just wanted to get her off his back and he had the power to do that. Joan appeared to have been happy with the sexual situation in their marriage at the time but subsequently it came out that Joan had been very unhappy at times and had considered leaving Bill.

Rick and Amanda

Rick had been a pornography addict for many years. He continually struggled to abstain from Internet pornography but predictably relapsed every time. He lead a deprived life in which he worked at a job for which he was over-qualified and over-educated, lived in a small studio apartment which he seldom cleaned, and had few real friendships. He had been an underearner for many years and had academic, musical, literary and other talents that he stopped pursuing. He ate poorly and had health problems which he neglected.

Rick's spare time after work was usually spent at the local coffee shop where he did some of his work on a laptop and had casual social contacts with the regulars at the coffee shop. He was friendly and could be agreeable and charming. When an attractive, usually much younger woman waited on him or chatted with him in passing, he was pleasant and appropriate, and they generally liked him. His typical pattern was to become attracted and occasionally fixated on one of these casual acquaintances and to fantasize about having a relationship with her. Almost as soon as he began obsessing about someone he would decide that it was probably hopeless to think about it and basically wallow in self-pity and self putdowns. In this mood he would return home later in the evening and act out with Internet pornography. This would often keep him up 'til all hours and he would be tired the next day and neglect his life even more.

In addition to Internet pornography, Rick engaged in phone sex with people he struck up phone acquaintances with but never met. He had one "friend," Amanda, with whom he had had such a phone relationship for years. He knew all about her life, her family, her relationship with her mother, her relationship with her various boyfriends over the years, and her health problems. He was a good listener, but the phone conversations consisted predominantly of sex talk. They both reverted to phone sex even when they had decided not to do so. Amanda told Rick that she felt turned on as soon as she heard his voice on the other end of the line. Through all these years Rick and Amanda never met in person.

Rick's phone sex habit escalated abruptly at one point when he lied to Amanda and told her he had started seeing someone. He also said that his "new girlfriend" was interested in a three-way with Amanda. Amanda was hesitant, as she had been extremely resistant to ever meeting Rick up to this point. Rick continued the lie and told Amanda that his girlfriend would pay Amanda to have sex with them. This was ultimately just let drop. Rick told someone in his support group about the lie to Amanda, and about the whole relationship. The friend was so alarmed at the possibility that Rick might ultimately get himself in trouble that Rick decided it was time to end the relationship with Amanda once and for all.

Rick and Amanda's Relationship Style

This is clearly an example of the Un-Relationship style. Rick's sex and relationship life existed on a fantasy plane as did his sexual acting out behavior. Although a bright and interesting person, in many ways he neglected himself and his life to the extent that he was actually incapable of attracting a girlfriend. His daily ritual brought up his feelings of inadequacy and shame and led him back home to acting out. His attempts at relationships were so frightening that they were kept at a distance and pursued only in fantasy. Rick had made several attempts to set up a meeting with Amanda (she lived in a nearby town) which always ended up getting cancelled by one of them. In one instance Rick became serious about meeting Amanda, believing that if they actually met it would break the spell, for better or for worse. But unsurprisingly, Amanda failed to come and failed to call. The lack of a real person in his life meant there was no obstacle to Rick's continued addiction.

Obviously many people have relationships that are hybrids or combinations of different styles. Think about your typical relationship style in the past and what features might be your own individual pattern. You will use this information in completing the Relationship Inventory in Chapter IV.

III. Identifying How You Choose a Partner

*The part of your brain that directed your search for a
mate, however, was not your logical, orderly new brain; it
was your time-locked, myopic old brain. And what your
old brain was trying to do was recreate the conditions of
your upbringing, in order to correct them.*

Harville Hendrix, *Getting the Love you Want*

When addicts choose a partner they tend to choose
someone who will allow them to continue to pursue their
addictions. This is usually happening on an *unconscious
level*; therefore, we say that *in your addiction, your
"addict" does the choosing of a partner.*

In recovery, the person's "addict" *still* wants to do the
choosing, i.e., this is a deeply engrained pattern. In order
to choose differently you will need to consciously deny
your "addict" what it wants. Only the choice of a new
kind of partner will allow you to practice stable and
intimate ways of relating and to change your relationship
style to one that promotes healthy closeness.

What follows are just a few of the many possible
examples of different kinds of people addicts might
choose as partners or spouses and the ways that such types
of people might, through no fault of their own, allow the
addict to continue in the addiction. ***There is not***

necessarily anything wrong with the partner types described below per se, but it is what they signify to the addict that is useful to look at. These are examples of some of the most obvious types and there are undoubtedly many, many more different and subtle kinds of addictive partner choices that you can think about. These are intended to be used as a starting point for you to define and analyze your own unique variations on a theme.

A Word About Accountability and Starting over with a Prior Relationship or Marriage

Many recovering sex addicts get into recovery because their addiction is discovered by a spouse or partner. In fact many addicts seek treatment and maintain their motivation to continue in recovery and stay sexually sober out of a feeling of being accountable to their spouse or partner. This can be a very good thing in the sense that it supports the addict's efforts in recovery, but it should not be the only reason the addict is in recovery.

If the addict's only reason to get into treatment or to stay in recovery is to "keep my wife happy," it is unlikely either that they will have a happy relationship or that the addict will stay in good recovery. In this situation the addict is making his or her recovery about someone else, and the motivation is to placate a partner rather than to actually recover and have a healthy relationship.

This lack of internal motivation means that the addict may not have a good enough basis for staying sober in the long run. It also means that the relationship will be continuing on the basis of what is likely to be an unhealthy relationship style, namely a parent-child style in which the addict must keep the spouse or partner convinced that they are being "good." As we will discuss further in Chapter VII, this is itself a form of co-dependence that addicts are prone to.

That said, many addicts find that their partnership and family are a very strong reason to do the work. Addicts may have *within themselves* the wish to make things right in their relationship, and that internal motivation is a positive source of accountability for them.

In starting over with the same partner, the addict will also have to look at the things that originally motivated the choice of that partner, and make a conscious effort to change those patterns of interacting that fed into their addiction in the past. They may find that once they have significantly changed their style, their partner will also be drawn into healthier ways of relating. Or they may openly ask their partner to help change the old roles for new ones.

The Unreliable Partner

The person prone to the High Drama relationship style may choose someone who is *unreliable*. The unreliable person may be seen as fascinating, a "free spirit," or a "damaged" person. They will seem special in some way: a rebel, a tortured genius, a heroic survivor, etc. This may seem like part of their charm at first, i.e., it may add to the feeling of fear and intensity. With 20/20 hindsight, one will be able to see that the "unreliable" person is also one who is prone to dishonesty, self-centeredness, manipulation and betrayal.

So why are addicts drawn to "unreliable" people? Well, they are well suited to live out the High Drama lifestyle in which there is mistrust, fear, intensity, conflict, break-ups, getting back together again, and more of the same. The relationship most likely begins impulsively with a very intense sexual attraction and little consideration of what may come next. Without reliability there is no room for stability, only chaos. With constant chaos there is no time for building an intimate bond.

How the Unreliable Partner Supports the Addiction

First and foremost, the chaotic nature of relating to someone who is unreliable tends to justify the addict's own lack of commitment and accountability. If you want to behave in a risky, selfish or exploitive way, then you have a built-in excuse in that your partner is so unpredictable or crazy that you can respond in kind. In fact, the unreliable partner may turn out to be sexually addictive in their own way. Thus, once the initial fantasy-fueled sexual attraction has subsided, both partners can perpetuate a situation in which sexual gratification exists largely outside of the relationship, and bonding and intimacy are compromised. Both people may know about each other's addictive acting out or they may engage in "triangulating," compulsively flirting or cheating with other people and so on. This is ultimately complicated and painful for both people, but it allows them to go on compartmentalizing their sexuality and using their acting out to maintain distance between them and their partner.

If the unreliable partner is of the needy and damaged type, then the addict can see him or her as "high maintenance." This is also a built-in excuse for the addict to lead a separate life and to feel justified in meeting his or her sexual needs outside the relationship. Feeling that he/she is safe from abandonment because the needy partner is so dependent keeps the addict feeling important. It also keeps the addict in a state of low-grade anger and resentment which further justifies his or her lack of accountability and over-entitlement.

The Checked-Out Partner

Sometimes the addict may consciously choose a partner in whom they have very minimal sexual interest, but who is willing to enter into the relationship or marriage anyway. Such addicts are often aware that they are doing something for quite cynical reasons and usually hold a view either that the relationship or marriage is not that big a deal—for example they may cite the fact that most married people are unfaithful anyway so attraction doesn't matter—or they may commit to the relationship for other manipulative, utilitarian reasons of their own. Either way they are engaged in a bad faith project in which their lack of integrity will undermine their self-concept even more.

How the Checked-out Partner Supports the Addiction

The relationship with the checked-out partner is one of very little closeness or emotional intimacy, even though it may not seem this way on the surface. Each person is living their own separate life without sharing their innermost self. This makes perfect sense since the addict can then pursue a secret life of sexual acting out and the partner will remain oblivious, leading their own life and largely ignoring what the addict does or doesn't do. Since they do not require much of each other, the partners do not challenge or confront one another. They may be feeling unfulfilled at a deeper level, but they lack the awareness and skills to try to enhance their relationship. To the question "Is this all there is?" these partners say "yes," and they mean it. The checked-out partners I have seen have often been the "workaholic" type, numbing out with work and looking to their work for their identity and self-worth. The addict seeks the false sense of connection and the fantasy of self-worth through sexual behaviors. Both partners are outwardly content and deeply lonely.

Sometimes the checked-out partner finds out about the addiction. At that point they may feel deeply betrayed, but this can be in large part because the addiction violates the checked-out partner's image of what they thought their relationship or marriage was. In other words the checked-out partner is not subject to the drama of heartbreak and betrayal to the same degree as other partners might be. Rather, they are wracked by the shame of not having a perfect marriage after all. The checked-out partner can thus be very narcissistic in his or her own way. This also serves the addict well. Even if the partner finds out about the addict's sexual betrayal, he or she may respond by minimizing it, wanting to wish it away or wanting to help find a quick "fix."

The Fleeting or Fantasy Partner

Short of not having a partner at all, a common pattern for sex addicts is to have fleeting relationships that do not go on very long or become very serious. The addict's intimacy problems are such that once the demands of a relationship go beyond a certain point, he or she tends to feel overwhelmed, or even panicked, and to flee. Lacking the basic relationship skills, and finding more intense gratification and greater safety in the context of their sexual acting out behavior, addicts cannot form a bond with a partner except in fantasy. They often engage in serial seductions or just flirtations.

Sometimes the fleeting partner is the partner encountered in sexual chat rooms or phone calls where there is intense fantasy to fuel the sexual encounter without any real mundane requirements impinging. These relationships can persist over years with the "partners" actually getting to know quite a lot about each other without ever meeting. This can give the illusion that the addict has a real relationship with the phone pal although there will often be extreme resistance to actually meeting the person.

Another common form of fantasy or "partial" relationship is the person the addict gets together with from time to time in order to have sex. There is little contact outside of these sexual encounters and although they persist over time, they are not real or intimate relationships in the usual sense. The choice of such partners generally has more of the features of sexual acting out than it has of a relationship. Phone pals and sex buddies fit into a category I consider to be a form of pseudo relationship. These may include some intense connections with friends, co-workers or relatives.

When you consider your relationship history in the coming chapters you will have to use your judgment as to what counts as a relationship for you.

How the Fleeting or Fantasy Partner Supports the Addiction

A relationship that exists only in fantasy is not a real relationship. Almost by definition, these fantasy relationships are *part of the addict's sexual acting out behavior.* What is often less obvious is that the fleeting relationships or seductions—the intrigue, the predatory flirting—are all part of a pattern of fantasy sexual acting out behavior. In effect the fleeting relationships often support the addiction because they are part of it.

On the other hand, the addict who has a separate sexual compulsion—say, Internet pornography—may also have flirtations and truncated relationships. Their real urge is to continue to pursue the addictive behavior—whatever that is—but they may also have a need to appear "normal" to their friends or themselves. All addicts have mixed feelings about having any real intimate relationship, and many have underlying anger toward women or men as the case may be. They may be capable of being charming and seductive and may take pleasure in feeling the sense of power that comes with a conquest. But they have a tendency to want to objectify the other person and so to distance themselves. Fairly quickly, the need to distance overtakes the need to seduce, and the addict withdraws. Thus they avoid the consequences of an involvement and go back to their addiction.

Sometimes the fleeting or fantasy partner is part of a pattern that fits the idea of "love addiction." The love addict may compulsively seduce people and begin relationships in which they are over-involved in a delusional way. They are subject to being devastated again and again in a vicious circle.

The fleeting partner is often perceived as "better" than the addict and this can be very intimidating and cause the addict to instantly withdraw. Paradoxically, the addict has adopted a very high standard of desirability, but when they encounter a highly desirable person their low self-concept will not allow them to feel confident enough to approach them in more than a casual way. Again and again they retreat, feeling deflated and taking comfort in addictive acting out.

Other Partner Choices

There are many other types of partners who may support your addiction in various ways, such as:

- A partner who serves as a rescuer,
- A partner who serves as a policeman,
- A companion who has no expectation of sex or romance, or
- A partner who is a combination of types.

There is a high degree of overlap between these types of partner choices, just as there is overlap between relationship styles. Partner choices may be a combination of types, and partner choices may shift over time during the addict's life pre-recovery.

Think about what kinds of partners or pseudo partners you have typically chosen (even if they do not fit the types described above), and think about how they supported your addiction in the past. You will use this information, along with your thoughts about your relationship style, when you complete your Relationship Inventory in the next chapter.

IV. Your Relationship Inventory

If you want to know your own mind, there is only one way:
to observe and recognize everything about it.

Thich Nhat Hanh, *The Miracle of Mindfulness*

Now that you have thought about your relationships and your choices of partners in your past life as a sex addict, you have a basis for understanding how your particular patterns supported a lifestyle of sexual acting out behavior. Use what you know up to this point to fill in some of the details about your relationship life in the past. Use the Relationship Inventory outline below to give as full a description as you can.

Then, formulate your typical relationship scenario so that you will have a clear idea of what the pitfalls were, and may still be, as you approach a new relationship in recovery.

Lastly, complete a relationship timeline to look at how your relationships progressed over time. You have not stopped living and growing, despite whatever problems you were dealing with. *You have been a thinking person and a part of you has wanted to get it right all along.* You have tried different things at different times and some of them may have been giant leaps forward in your understanding of what you needed to do to relate in a healthier way.

Relationship Inventory

1. List all the dating or other romantic relationships you have had regardless of how they turned out. List them in order from earliest to latest, and give the time period they lasted and your age, including where they overlapped. Do not include brief encounters with prostitutes, massage workers, baristas etc. unless you became preoccupied with one of them in fantasy or attempted to form a connection with one of them. Do include relationships with chat or phone partners and sexual acting out partners (e.g. sex buddies) if they went on for some time (i.e. more than a few weeks).

Relationship	Time Period in Your Life

Now describe some *typical characteristics* of your relationship history such as short vs. long relationships, more than one relationship at a time, becoming obsessed with someone without actually getting into a relationship, etc. Include your opinion of how this pattern may have changed over time, e.g. did you become more isolated? Did you have more self-destructive relationships? Etc.

_____

_____

_____

_____

_____

_____

_____

_____

_____

_____

_____

2. For each relationship on your list briefly describe how it started:

❖ Who initiated the relationship?

❖ What things got you interested? What was the hook?

❖ Were you similar in age?

❖ Were you similar in level of life accomplishments or success?

❖ Were you similar in financial resources?

Who Initiated?	Relative Success?	The "Hook"?	Financial?	Relative Age?

Now look over these answers and describe the most common pattern by which you became interested in someone and connected with them. Include the most frequently occurring *characteristics of your partner choices.*

_____

_____

_____

_____

_____

_____

_____

_____

3. Describe the process of getting to know each of the people on your list:

❖ What did you do together while getting acquainted?
❖ What interests and activities did you have in common?

Process of Getting Acquainted	Interests and Activities Shared

Now look over these answers and describe your most *typical pattern* of pursuing some kind of relationship:

_____

_____

_____

_____

_____

_____

_____

_____

_____

_____

_____

_____

4. For each person on your list describe your **sex life** together:

❖ Who initiated sex or tried to?

❖ What was your level of sexual interest in the person?

❖ Did you talk about having sex before you began having sex?

❖ Did you have any basic understandings between you about sex?

How Sex Started	Your Level of Interest	Talked Beforehand?	Shared Ideas Re: Sex?

Now look at these answers and describe your sexual style in relationships. For example, were you usually having sex with your partner but thinking of something else? Was there an atmosphere of sexual mistrust and suspicion? Did you use your partner sexually in some way? Did you attempt to bring your addictive acting out behavior into the sexual relationship with your partner (e.g. acting out roles, watching porn together, wanting to bring third parties into the act, using sex toys to further your fantasies, etc.)?

_____

_____

_____

_____

_____

_____

_____

_____

_____

5. For each relationship on your list give a brief description of the way you interacted with each other:

   ❖ How did you share your feelings?

   ❖ How did you solve problems?

   ❖ What underlying roles did you play in relation to each other (e.g. father, wayward child, ships in the night, etc?)

Expression of Feelings	Problem-Solving Process	Roles You Played

5. Now describe the day-to-day feeling between you and whomever you were involved with. Did you typically avoid any self-revelation? Did you placate or give in to your partner, only to feel resentment? Did you avoid each other? Was there emotional or physical violence?

_____

_____

_____

_____

_____

_____

_____

6. For each relationship describe how the relationship ended:

- ❖ Who ended it, and how?
- ❖ Was it on-again-off-again?
- ❖ Was it left unresolved?

Who Ended the Relationship?	On-and-Off but Never Ended?	Parted Without Clarity?

Now describe what you see as your typical way of ending a relationship:

_____

_____

_____

_____
_____
_____
_____
_____
_____
_____
_____
_____

7. Based on descriptions you wrote for the six questions above write a brief description of your typical relationship scenario.

Examples of Relationship Scenarios:

(a) "I was initially very attracted to someone who usually turned out to be someone who became too dependent. I felt that the relationship would help me stop my pattern of going to strip clubs and massage parlors, but I sooner or later resumed this pattern in secret. In the course of the relationship I played the role of the good lover and partner, but I cared less and less for this person. I felt that sexual acting out was my legitimate outlet. There were a lot of crises and a lot of arguments and I always ended up placating my partner. I would feel resentful and look for a way to get out of the relationship, often cheating and openly flirting with other people. If I felt a partner was unhappy and threatening to leave, I would break up with them first in order to avoid having to confront any issues. I was never able to be honest about what was really going on with me."

(b) "I chose a partner because I thought they 'looked good on paper.' They were attractive and accomplished and they seemed to love me, but I was not actually attracted to them. I knew all along that I would probably continue to have a separate sexual life involving anonymous sexual encounters and voyeurism. We would have a relationship that seemed outwardly OK and we would get along well for the most part. There were always many things in my past that I never told my partner and that I was very ashamed of. I always felt 'less than' and my sexual acting out made me feel worse. I was depressed but I didn't talk about it. Over time I got careless and my acting out got more bizarre. I wanted to change something but I didn't know how."

(c) "I was always romantically obsessed with some person even in high school but it never worked out. I always got rejected or felt humiliated in some way. I was increasingly interested in my secret sexual fantasy life of Internet pornography. I would continue to develop fantasies about people at work or on the street and would sometimes try to strike up an acquaintance with an extremely attractive person. Once or twice I had brief dating situations, but it was all about sex and they were not ever real prospects for bonding or forming a partnership. I never really thought about how to go about meeting appropriate people and never considered what I had to offer someone as a friend or lover—only what I wanted. I resented the fact that I could not have a partner who measured up to my fantasies, and felt sorry for myself. I was in a self-perpetuating rut and didn't have any idea how to proceed."

My Relationship Scenario:

_____

_____

_____

_____

_____

_____

_____

_____

_____

_____

_____

_____

My Relationship Timeline: The Things I Got Right

Now give yourself some credit. Now that you have looked at the set-up for relationships not working, go back over your relationships in chronological order and think about where you attempted to do things better, where you did in fact make changes that mattered even if you still struggled with some basic issues. Recognize that you, like all humans, have a basic drive toward health and growth. You always get some things right.

_____

_____

_____

_____

_____

_____

_____

_____

_____

_____

_____

_____

Times I Thought it was Going to be Different:

Examples: I picked someone I thought was mentally healthier; I made a decision to commit to a partner in a deeper way; I decided to get into couple counseling; I decided to start a family; I looked for a relationship not built around sex.

1. _____

2. _____

3. _____

4. _____

Ways I Got it Right(er):

Examples: I got sober in AA; I got on a better footing financially; I felt some real love and connection with someone; I developed some supports in the community.

1. _____

2. _____

3. _____

Ways It Was the Same Old Scenario:

Examples: I was still deceptive and dishonest; I was unable to express my needs in a balanced way; I was still depressed and felt unsuccessful and unlovable; I still acted out my addictions in secret.

1. _____

2. _____

3. _____

4. _____

As you look at your typical relationship scenario, observe how things were arranged around your addictive acting out behavior as well as how things evolved or improved in some ways. Make a list of the problems with the old style, the most important characteristics of that scenario that need to change. You can use these in completing the worksheets in Chapter VIII and the Relapse Scenario in Chapter XII. Next to that list make a list of things you would ideally like to do differently and how that would look, even if it seems impossible right now.

Example:

Problems with Old Relationship Style	Vision for New Relationship Style
I was too ashamed of myself to be open or honest about what I needed. I just stored up resentments and acted out instead.	Feeling good about myself and feeling safe sharing who I really am and trusting someone to be responsive and caring.
I always felt mired in conflict and reacted with sarcasm and aggression when I was afraid I couldn't get my needs met.	Feeling centered and calm and approaching differences with a spirit of cooperation and good will.
Staying very busy so that I wouldn't have to spend time with my partners	Valuing the time together with someone and feeling happy doing things together or just doing nothing together.
I always felt a relationship was tenuous and would end badly. I protected myself by holding back.	Investing in a relationship and allowing myself to commit to a future with someone.

In the next chapter we will pause to take a look at the early childhood issues that lead to addiction and intimacy disability. In the remaining chapters we will talk about tools for changing relationship patterns and the challenges and recovery solutions involved in finding and maintaining an intimate relationship.

V. Understanding How It All Started

...That part of a child which is traumatized or threatened refuses to grow older. The rest of the psyche may grow and mature, closing like a protective callus around the wound, but the wound itself remains isolated. This wound is more often than not located in a specific part of the body, one that can no longer speak.

David Whyte, *The Heart Aroused*

Origins in Infant and Childhood Bonding Problems

People are drawn to addictive rather than healthy relationships for reasons relating to their early family life. Sexual addiction as an intimacy disorder results in part from a lack of adequate bonding due to some disruption in the relationship to a primary caregiver (usually the parent). Appropriate non-verbal "inter-subjective" relating between an infant and caregiver has proven to be crucial for brain development and has a major impact in the learning of emotion regulation, impulse control and the reward systems of the brain (Schore, 1994). These subtle, interpersonal attachment traumas in infancy lead to problems with emotional and behavioral control, and ultimately to addictions and impaired ability to trust and bond normally with another person.

In their childhood many sex addicts were sexually and/or physically abused, but they were as likely, or more likely, to have been emotionally neglected. Also they very frequently come from families in which the caregivers are disengaged, rigid, authoritarian or sexually repressed. Both the early attachment trauma and the later experience of inadequate parenting in childhood contribute not only to the susceptibility to addiction but to the inability to form normal relationships later in life.

In sex addicts this intimacy disorder leads to the addict leading a "double life." Most often all or part of the addict's *sex life* exists apart from his or her life with a spouse, partner, boyfriend or girlfriend. Even when the sex addict is having sex with a partner or spouse, it is often the case that the addict is not "all there." He or she may be lost in fantasy or just going through the motions. Many addicts feel they are having satisfying sex with their partners when in fact they are not really able to be present mentally or emotionally. Even addicts who feel they really desire their partner usually have some other more compelling and highly charged experience that they revert to outside of their relationship whether it is serial seduction, hook-ups, prostitutes, chat rooms or affairs.

One sex addict I know had an active and good sex life alongside his acting out behavior (exhibitionism). Obviously all the good sex he was getting with appropriate women partners was not helping him to keep from acting out on the side. He married an extremely attractive woman and had a seemingly normal relationship with her, but his fantasy life during sex was occupied with his acting out scenarios, and he still was not abstinent from his addictive behaviors which were becoming more extreme.

He finally got into recovery (due to getting found out) and got sober from sexual acting out.

The untreated baggage of a disordered attachment history leads to mistrust, fear, distancing, sexual conflicts, feeling unlovable, and lack of experience with healthy communication. These are the problems that support the splitting off of part of oneself in sex addiction. Sex addicts are cut off from true intimacy with another and are equally cut off from themselves. They have developed a life-long habit of avoiding feelings because of the need to "wall off" early painful feelings as a child. Without access to their inner feelings, addicts are not able to reflect on what they are doing and its consequences, leading to impulsive behavior aimed at escape. Becoming aware of feelings is anathema to many addicts. Some will even tell you that the mere idea of intimacy with another person evokes the immediate thought of pain. Addicts have to learn how to observe, identify and evaluate their own emotions and it is not easy for them. One addict in a therapy group admitted to having been so oblivious of his feelings that, he said: "I used to think that 'hunger' was a feeling."

Dr. Patrick Carnes has said that "The starting point for all trauma survivors is a complete acceptance of the betrayal" (Carnes, 1997). The process of accepting that we have been damaged and allowing ourselves to experience and expel the feelings connected with those damaging experiences may not happen all at once or be completed in the early stages of recovery.

Likewise, the relational trauma beginning in infancy and causing the neuropsychological damage to the addict's self-regulatory and reward systems can be repaired by the positive attachment experiences in the relationships experienced through therapy, treatment and support groups.

Connecting the dots between our parents' dysfunction and our later relationship dysfunction

When the developing child is cared for by parental figures who are deficient in relating intimately to another person, that deficiency not only affects the child in terms of their very early neurological deficits, it also affects their experience of intimate relationships while growing up. I conceive of three main routes through which parents who are damaged in their intimate relating with a partner, with their children and in general can communicate and instill the same intimacy disability in their children. These routes are:

1. Modeling

2. Disengagement

3. Exploitation

Modeling

In modeling the child learns through direct observation that the most intimate adult relationship is full of dishonesty and dissatisfaction. Although their parents may have played the role of the "happy couple," their marriage may have been unfulfilled, estranged or empty of real closeness. Or the parents may have been openly unhappy and in conflict. In such situations, the children have *no model of a healthy, happy marriage.* Having no direct knowledge of what a love relationship between adults should look like, the child grows up with an expectation of relationships as fraudulent, unsafe, and lacking in real devotion. As children grow up they may become dimly aware that some people seem to be happily married, but as far as any direct knowledge of this state of affairs goes, it might as well not exist. They cannot even imagine what, to them, is a blank concept.

Therefore, in addition to whatever damage is done to the child by the parent's inadequate parenting of the child, the child's future relating as an adult will be in some way a replication or reaction to the behavior of the caregivers with one another. The lesson learned by observing intimacy-disabled parents can become a relationship template for the child later in life. The child may learn through observation that intimacy is dirty and should be hidden, that intimate relationships are full of danger and violence and should be avoided or, as is the case with children of sex addicts, that partner relationships are not where their parent's true passion and sexual interest lies. The possible messages that can be internalized in this way are many. The child will grow up with some warped idea of what a partnership is; for example, it is "pain," or "shame," or "secrecy," or it is "tense formality."

Having a normal model of intimacy as a child would make future relating to a partner a lot less frightening and mysterious. Imagine if we had had parents who were consistent in their relationship; who were affectionate, kind and devoted toward one another; who were open with their love and never derisive or mean-spirited. How much easier it would have been if we could have been able to model our behavior on that kind of template.

Disengagement

Parents who are lacking in intimacy skills in their own marriage not only fail at nurturing each other, they also most likely fail to interact with and nurture their children in appropriate ways. Parental disengagement results in emotional neglect; children suffer from the feeling that no one will be there when they need them, or that their caregivers don't "get" them. Seeking support or nurturance from such caregivers is disappointing and/or hurtful.

These children grow up to be addicts partly because they needed a way to provide for themselves the soothing, regulating function that was not being provided by their emotionally unavailable or unsupportive parents.

This is true regardless of the form that the parental unavailability takes, such as absence due to death or illness, outright abuse, abandonment, over-indulgence or "smothering." People who are prone to addictive or unhealthy relationships are most often people who learned NOT to expect other people to be there in a healthy way.

I have observed that it is a fairly common experience in sex addicts to feel like they are invisible as children, or as wanting to make themselves invisible. This could be a reaction to feeling that they are ignored, or it could be a defense against the rejection and "mis-attunement" they anticipate in relating to their caregivers. These are the children who are expected to be "seen and not heard," or maybe not even seen.

Exploitation

Exploitation happens when people whose parents were incapable of a healthy relationship rely on their children in unhealthy ways. Such parents "use" their children to provide emotional outlets or emotional supports that are lacking in their marriage. Parents may vent their frustrations on their children; they may make their children into "confidantes"—burdening them with their own problems—or they may cast their children in the role of a boyfriend/girlfriend or surrogate partner. The latter is sometimes referred to as "role-reversal." Exploitation is a common pattern of parenting experienced by a majority of addicts and codependents. The message is one destined to promote unhealthy core beliefs about one's worth as a person. The message is, *"My value as a person depends on my value to someone else."*

Role-reversal and any inappropriate way of relying on a child can have the consequence of making the child see themselves as objects of utility for another. Using and being used, proving one's worth by being desirable and/or seductive, and acting out the resulting anger and resentment by serial seduction or by using other people in return are some of the resulting processes which cause problems in the person's way of relating later on.

Dr. Kenneth M. Adams has written extensively about the often subtle processes of exploitation and their dire consequences in terms of relationships and sex addiction. 'Emotional incest,' as it is sometimes called, is often difficult to spot, especially for the growing child, and especially if the child is a boy. Adams' books are excellent sources for those who feel that they may have had sexually violating or sexually intrusive experiences as a child but who are not sure exactly what form it took (Adams, K. M., 2011; Adams, K.M. & Morgan A.P., 2007).

Not all problems with attachment in childhood and the resulting intimacy disorders come from a parent's emotional disability. Some attachment problems also arise through accidents of fate such as the illness, absence or death of a caregiver. (There is also thought to be both a genetic contribution to addictions in general which may be passed on as a predisposition to addiction in the case of sexual addiction as well.) But given a child of average resiliency, it is now believed that the effects of the trauma or loss suffered through accidents of fate or outside influences, although serious, are *significantly mitigated or exaggerated* depending on whether the caregivers' responses are protective, supportive and validating or the opposite. The right kind of support and nurturance in the time of the trauma can go a long way toward preventing any long-lasting psychological damage by restoring safety and trust in significant others.

Examples from Real Life (no real names used)

<u>Tom</u>

Modeling: Tom is a 50-year-old sex addict who came from a family with parents who did not exhibit any closeness in their relating and were often at odds. In fact, Tom's father was competitive with Tom and tried to outdo him in any achievements or attributes that Tom had as a kid. Tom's mother covertly played into this "triangle" between herself, Tom and Tom's father. Tom grew up with no sense of a normal adult love relationship and felt that his father was ridiculous and pathetic. Tom felt he was smarter than both his parents and decided at a very early age that he would have to go it alone.

Disengagement: Tom's mother was self-centered, and his father was emotionally immature. His mother was controlling and expected her children to please her and meet her needs. Tom's father was so easily threatened that he constantly disapproved of Tom just to prove himself. Tom was not supported or accepted for who he was and felt that he had to conceal his true self. He developed a façade of sociability and never felt really safe around people.

Exploitation: Tom's family lived in a home that was laid out such that he had to walk through his parents' bedroom to get to the only bathroom. He felt that there was something inappropriate about his mother's attention to him but could never put his finger on it. His mother used Tom as a primary support instead of Tom's father. This made Tom into a partner rather than a son. When there was a family crisis relating to Tom's brother, Tom's mother went to Tom and cried on his shoulder as Tom's father looked on. Tom developed a pornography addiction early in his teens. He has never been able to maintain any relationship with a woman. He objectifies women and is aware of having anger at them. He admits to feeling fear around getting too close to women and he feels this fear is related to the danger he felt from his father for getting too close to his mother.

Dick

Modeling: Dick is in his 40s and has his own small business. Dick's parents were alcoholics, and Dick remembers a lot of drinking and arguing. They were not happy together, but Dick's mother said that since she worked full time she felt had to stay with Dick's father even though he cheated on her. After Dick entered treatment for sex addiction, his mother disclosed that she had been molested as a child. Both parents were unable to express or accept love, and Dick learned to be shut down in relationships. He was uncomfortable in social situations later on and became an alcoholic. He married a woman who "saved" him, and they both got sober in AA. She became a parent/ disciplinarian figure. Alongside this marriage Dick's sex addiction escalated, leading to more extreme behaviors and several arrests.

Disengagement:

Dick got no nurturance or support from his parents. By age three he was told never to cry. If he had a problem he did not go to his parents. His father hit him frequently beginning about age five. Dick learned never to express his feelings, and he began to try in every way to be a pleaser. As an adolescent he began to lead a double life and began being sexually compulsive. He has never been able to assert himself or to express his anger appropriately. He is currently taking parenting classes and feels he is gaining a lot of insight into himself and is learning to be there for his four-year-old daughter. He is also in therapy and 12-Step treatment.

Exploitation:

Dick feels that growing up he and his siblings were there to serve their parents. His father is now dead, but his mother still expects Dick and his siblings to visit her and spend their time doing work for her. As a boy, Dick was molested repeatedly during the summers by a male neighbor. He did not tell his mother, but he was always hesitant to visit with the neighbor and Dick's mother would urge him to go anyway. Dick became rebellious as soon as he could get away from his parents. He acted out his anger in extreme rebellion and sexual acting out. Dick never had the feeling that he controlled his own life and lacked an internal locus of control in the extreme. He feels that he is two different people; he experiences his addictive self as almost having a life of its own.

Harry

Modeling:

Harry got into recovery in his 50s. He grew up in a family in which both parents were deaf. Harry and his older sister had normal hearing. There was little healthy relating between Harry's parents with much conflict and a lack of warmth and cohesiveness. Harry's family lived in cramped quarters in a small apartment. There was a lack of appropriate boundaries. Harry married a woman who saw Harry as a "project" and wanted to "fix" him. Harry expressed his anger and resentment in sexual acting out for many years. He was able to be a good and devoted parent to two children, but he and his workaholic wife were often like ships passing at night.

Disengagement:

Harry had an extremely abnormal early attachment history due to the fact that his parents could not hear him. His sister was able to respond to him and mitigated the situation to some degree. Harry's mother had difficulty being emotionally supportive to her children and tended to deal with their upsets by giving them food, which helped promote an eating disorder in the sister. The mother was also very emotionally volatile and would alternately smother Harry and then fly off the handle and beat him for no reason. Harry's father was not able to be supportive and would childishly undercut Harry's goals and achievements. Harry began acting out sexually in the form of exposing himself starting at age thirteen.

Exploitation:

Harry's parents were both immature and needy in their own ways. They both lacked emotional as well as physical boundaries and were oblivious to some of the standards of appropriate behavior. While Harry was still but a child, his parents, his mother in particular, relied on him to an inordinate degree for such day-to-day communication and household needs as answering the phone or going to the store. Both parents' negative attitudes and guilt trips lead to Harry feeling an extreme lack of self worth and low expectations in life despite his being very bright. He continued his sexual addiction in several different forms into adulthood. He dropped out of college and joined a "therapeutic community" in which having healthy relationships was defined as having sex with as many different members as possible and never confining oneself to a couple relationship.

Why Trauma Resolution Helps Relationships

Most people in addiction recovery will be familiar with these ideas. In the simplest terms, addicts relate to others in their disabled way because they continue to rely upon the defense mechanisms they learned in childhood. These are sometimes called "survival skills that no longer serve." If it was not safe to trust others—if we were stressed or disappointed in seeking the love and closeness we needed in early life—we developed a coping mechanism that allowed us to survive in that situation, and upon which we continue to rely, however unhealthy it is to do so now.

Once we are grown up, we are free of the damaging influence, but we have a habitual way of responding that remains. We continue to try to escape our feelings, to protect ourselves from the "inevitable" hurt associated with intimate relationships and to prove ourselves to be lovable, powerful, or safe by acting out a variety of addictive, compulsive but basically unconscious behaviors.

In "working through" trauma we quite literally allow ourselves to feel the pain we are unconsciously defending against. Through one or another therapeutic intervention, we thaw out the "frozen feelings" we have forgotten. We reexperience, or maybe allow ourselves to fully experience for the first time, the original pain and stress that we were subjected to in childhood.

This reexperiencing does two things.

First, it allows us to grieve for ourselves, to grieve the loss of what we never had, and in grieving to finally put that loss to rest. We can stop expecting for some miracle to undo the past or repaint our childhood experiences in a better light. We can realize that there is no need to make excuses or explanations for what happened to us. We accept the reality of what happened; we accept that we were damaged by it; we accept that our past is never going to change. And we grieve.

Second, it allows us to let go of our "survival skills that no longer serve," and our "acting out defenses." Why? Because once we have felt the depth of the past pain, then the worst has happened! We have survived the feelings we were defending against and are now able to let go of the old defenses. We finally have some real evidence that we don't need to behave that way. Unless and until we go through this process—or rather to the extent that we have not completed this process—we will still be subject to our old fears, and our old defenses may creep back into our behavior.

Since the process of letting go of old survival strategies is one that may go on throughout our life as we grow stronger, we will undoubtedly have a tendency when under stress to revert to old behaviors to some extent. In addition, we will have to practice the new behaviors that allow us to trust and connect and get used to using them in real life. We cannot wait until we are perfect at this to begin trying to have an intimate relationship with another person. So we will need to prepare as best we can for the challenges that will come up along the way.

Early Trauma in a Relationship Context

In any relationship in recovery it will be important to pay close attention when strong reactions arise in relation to your partner. If you are feeling victimized, if you are nursing a grudge, if you are feeling intimidated or you are wanting to get even, you will first and foremost need to look at what automatic reactions from childhood may still be operating. This is not to say that your partner can't be genuinely annoying or overbearing at times, but when you react you become unconscious. When you are unconscious you have the potential to be carried away. Conversely, when you become aware that your reactions are being fueled by residual unconscious defenses, you have the potential to resolve the situation in a healthier way. If you are vigilant to your own reactions and can reflect on them, you have the potential to resolve them by virtue of what you know about your own history. *You can then remind yourself that the other person is not your father or your mother*, that you are not in any danger, and that your partner has a right to have emotions and so on.

It is vitally important that you listen to your partner about what is going on with you when you feel carried away. If your partner is baffled by your reaction it may be because they have a better perspective on it due to the fact that it doesn't really relate directly to them. Let their words sink in before you try to combat them. This is hard to do, but it is a lot easier to do when you can become aware that you are reacting from your history rather than from the present. If you are both having strong emotional reactions and blaming each other, then you may both be coming from an unconscious place, and you need to each *examine what is going on inside you separately from each other*. The midst of an irrational emotional exchange is no place to talk about and try to analyze what's really going on. In Chapters X and XII we will talk more about improving and using mindfulness skills to help you look at your own reactions rather than allowing them to throw you into your automatic unconscious mode.

With regard to situations between you and your family of origin there may be many unhealthy ways of relating that persist even up to the present time. You may have examined your conditioned responses from your early life, but other family members may not have had the benefit of growing and changing in this area. And even though you have an awareness of your family dynamics, you may have a hard time seeing the old patterns of relating and, as a result, you may still fall into old roles. If you were ignored or devalued by family members as a child, you may not notice that this is continuing to happen. If you were exploited, or your boundaries were violated as a child, your family may still be engaging in these behaviors in some form. Once again, your spouse or partner may be better able to see this than you. These old patterns of reacting hold you back, and you would do well to let someone help you to see them for what they are and learn to opt out of the old role.

VI. The New Paradigm:
Areas for Basic Change

*Paradigm: The most annoying and misused word
in the English language; used intentionally by stupid
people to sound smart or by smart people to sound
unintentionally stupid.*

Urban Dictionary

The word 'paradigm' also happens to be a useful one at
times. A paradigm is a closed set of accepted theories. A
paradigm is a model or pattern. It is also a set of ideas or
assumptions. It is also a mindset. So when we talk about
a new relationship paradigm, we are talking about changing our theories and assumptions about relationships and
looking at them in a new way. We are talking about basic
changes in what we think relationships are for, how we
think they originate and evolve, what we expect them to
require of us and how we imagine a "good" relationship to
look.

As we have talked about in the previous chapters, it is
sometimes easy to see that you have been in a rut or that
you have a self-defeating relationship script; it is often possible to see how that pattern was laid down by various influences in your early life. It is harder to get out of the box
you are in and think about what it would really be like to do
things differently.

The paradigm shift here refers in large part to a change in *what you think a relationship is for.* One reason addicts have trouble finding the right person and sustaining a stable relationship is that they have a distorted view of the function of a relationship in their life. Here are some examples:

- A relationship will bring me social recognition and acceptance in a world I want to belong to.

- A relationship with a glamorous person will make me proud and confident and make others envy me.

- A relationship with the right person will provide the perfect balance to my life.

- A committed relationship with children will make me a normal person with a normal life.

- We will be considered a "great looking couple."

- The right relationship can cure my addictions.

There are many such examples, but you get the idea. The shift involved is to some other view that has to do with the day-to-day realities of life within the relationship.

A recovering addict told me he was uncertain about whether to commit to a relationship with his girlfriend. He wasn't sure she was the right person; he was afraid, and so on. I asked him if he looked forward to going to the supermarket with his girlfriend and keeping house, etc. His jaw dropped. It was an aspect of relationships that he had not envisioned.

Another addict told me that he was desperately looking for a committed relationship but that he could not really see changing anything about the way he lived (he works all night at home and sleeps most of the day), or changing where he lived or anything else. There often appears to be a failure on the addict's part to imagine him or herself in a stable relationship. They can get as far as what they think might be a good "match" for them, but what comes after that is sometimes shrouded in mystery. This goes way beyond the inability to compromise. It is the inability to imagine a life together on a reality plane.

As you will see in Chapter XI, plenty of people have attempted to explain such a new paradigm in terms of a set of characteristics that are present in a "good" or "healthy" intimate relationship. These are all accurate descriptions ("speaking your truth in the moment," "respect," "cooperation," "nurturance") but they may be a foreign language to the recovering addict. Even if they made immediate sense, it is by no means immediately obvious how to get there. I believe you get there by allowing yourself to look at new ideas, new formulations about relationships and how they work in general and identifying ways you might begin to try doing something differently based on these new concepts.

New Paradigms: New Ways of Thinking

In the coming chapters you will hopefully be able to create your own program for change that is individually suited to you. In the meantime, here are some of the new ideas you might consider as you try to shift away from an old relationship style to a new and unfamiliar one. These "rules" are intended only to stimulate thinking and not as the final word on what is right or wrong.

1. Sexual attraction is not the main thing.

Many sex addicts use sexual attraction as a social filter. They decide who to approach based on sexual standards of looks and have no use for any interaction with less dazzling people. They *rationalize* this by saying that they *can't possibly be in a relationship with someone who does not meet some baseline level of sexual attractiveness.*

This sounds right, and yet it is true only in the most superficial sense. I have pointed out to addicts that they have probably been very sexually drawn to someone at some point in their lives only to find that when they got to know a little more about them, the attraction faded because of personality traits that made them *un*attractive.

So it can be that someone who seemed at first blush to be a great prize ended up seeming like a dud. By the same token, the addict needs to take a more open view of potential partners, admitting that a person who seems only somewhat attractive, attractive *enough* but not drop dead gorgeous, may end up being endlessly fascinating, the best thing that ever happened to them, a soul mate. *You don't know how attractive someone really is until you really get to know them.*

And just as a footnote, you have probably, in the course of your life and your attempted relationships, developed an idea of what your "type" is. This "type" of what an attractive person looks like or seems like is something you will need to learn to watch out for. We will discuss the issue of the feeling of "instant familiarity" in Chapter VIII when we talk about formulating a sober dating plan. As you grow in relationship recovery, your idea of your type may change in small or large ways too. This is because your priorities will change. In recovery you have already learned that *"pleasure won't make you happy."* As we will see in later chapters, relationships are there to bring many rewards, including pleasure. But they are also there for other reasons that may end up being more important to you.

2. Looking for your equal means being willing to get hurt.

Sex addicts often come from abusive or emotionally neglectful early childhood situations. They carry with them the unconscious need to **totally control all close relationships** so as to avoid what they expect and dread: that they will get hurt. This is what makes you as an addict seek out a relationship with a partner who is less powerful than you. It is safe to be with someone who needs you, who is weak, neurotic, poor, underachieving, or young.

But the only healthy relationship is a relationship of equals. If you are the one with all the power by whatever definition—financial, age, looks, fame etc.—it reassures you that your partner will not be able to reject you, abandon you or otherwise hurt you. Moving in the direction of a healthy relationship in recovery means that you accept the need to be with someone who is roughly equally independent, powerful and emotionally mature. This means they can, and probably will, at some point hurt you in some way. Healthy relationships are not 100 percent safe all the time.

When you enter into a relationship with an equal you accept that person at whatever stage of their development they have reached. You will need to have some basic trust in your partner's good intentions, but you will have to be willing for them to do things you don't like. You also have to accept that they are not perfect and never will be; they may act unconsciously, shut you out, or neglect the relationship at times. You will be able to deal with these situations to the extent that you have learned to trust that you can stay centered and say and do what will keep you from getting demolished by another person. A partner who is your equal will always be able to say or do hurtful things. Only by trusting your <u>own</u> ability to deal with situations in a mature way, to talk about what you feel and to set boundaries, will you be able to make relating to a partner safe.

3. Expect your relationship to meet 20% of your needs.

The above may seem like an overstatement, but it is meant to dramatize one of the paradigm shifts that many addicts in recovery must make. It is a new idea to most addicts that a relationship is not the answer to all their problems. No relationship can flourish under that kind of weight. By the same token, your own growth would be stultified in an all-consuming relationship. Even addicts who are afraid to get close to someone for fear of "engulfment" or loss of self fall into the trap of expecting a relationship with the "right person" to make their life OK. (We will hear more about the "not right person" idea in Chapter IX.)

It might seem ironic that sex addicts who have in the past invested only certain parts of themselves in their relationships and held a lot of themselves separate, should somehow at the same time believe that a good relationship will be all-encompassing and meet all their needs. A good relationship will likely be your most important and precious relationship, but it will not make your life OK if your life is not OK. In that sense it is only part of your larger life.

The fact that a relationship can only be expected to meet a certain percentage of your needs does not mean that you decline to engage in it with a hundred percent of yourself. In fact, an intimate relationship is the relationship where you will share all parts of yourself with your partner and be invested in a deeper way than in other relationships in your life.

When you as a recovering addict are no longer haunted by the fear of abandonment and have established a stronger sense of independence and self-worth, then you begin to find satisfaction and joy in life without a partner. At that point the relationship that you enter into will take its proper place in your life. It will be something to enjoy, learn from, and only sometimes struggle with. It will exist in a context of friends, family, and community. It may be the most central and important bond in your life, but you will be a person with many needs and many relationships that feed you in many other and different ways.

4. Security is not a dirty word.

There is a saying in recovery groups that for an addict *"Relationships are like putting Miracle-Gro^{TM} on your problems."* This is only true to the extent that the addict and his partner have not yet reached a point where they have adopted a different and healthier paradigm for relationships.

If your relationship style in your addiction was characterized by conflict and competition, dishonesty and secrecy, then when you begin to have relationships in recovery you may find these things rearing their heads again in a big way. As a person in recovery, you may feel you have committed to a life of surrender (to a Higher Power), of living "one day at a time," and of being of service to others. And this may work quite well until a potential partner comes along.

The self-centered, ego-driven life of the addict may have been brought to the light of consciousness through recovery, but an intimate relationship will likely draw out whatever residual fears remain, leading to all the turmoil and conflict of the old relationship style.

But it doesn't have to be this way. The problem with the clever saying about Miracle-Gro is that it should not be the norm. If, as a recovering addict, you have addressed the problems and the pathology inherent in your unhealthy way of conducting relationships in the past, and if your style has shifted, you will be ready to find a healthy partner and to form an intimate bond that is built upon *security, peace and cooperation.*

So what about another recovery slogan you may have heard, that *"Recovery is one step up from boring?"* There is a nugget of truth in this, but more so if viewed through the eyes of the un-recovered addict. Life in recovery and healthy relationships in recovery should be full of passion, adventure and fulfillment. "Boring" is just a way to make the point that the addict will have to settle for happiness, contentment and devotion most of the time instead of intrigue, danger and adrenaline.

5. If it's real, it's going to be scary.

Starting a relationship on a reality plane can be very frightening in the beginning. In addictive relationships you have much more control. This might seem paradoxical since many addicts will take great risks in pursuing their addictive behavior, such as risks of getting hurt, risks of getting in trouble with the law and risks of contracting diseases. But for many addicts these risks are nothing compared to how frightening it feels to seriously begin a relationship with someone where there is a potential for something real and lasting. One sex addict I treated admitted to being petrified of attempting to start a relationship with a partner who was strong and healthy, what he called the "right kind of woman," because that kind of relationship would be a leap into the unknown.

One recovering sex addict put it well when he said that in his addiction he always knew what was going to happen, it was always the same outcome. In your sexual acting out you are in essence finding a way to act out the same fantasy over and over. You orchestrate it, you control it. No sweat.

Even if the relationship is with a real person, a person who might have the potential to be a real partner, you as a practicing addict will not invest in that relationship and so you will have little to lose. You have little to lose because you have another life that you are invested in, your fantasy life, your acting out life.

This is even true if you are a love addict. Love addicts are obsessed with the love they have or the loss of it, but this is all going on in their head. It is their drama, and if there is any fear, it is the fear of not having a love object on which to project that obsession. They are in the same narcissistic bubble as any sex addict, and in this way all addicts keep themselves safe from experiencing the fear of actual connection and their fear of not measuring up.

By the same token, you could say, "If it's not scary it's not real." I suspect that normal people know this and are thus better prepared. For you as an addict the fear of the unknown and the sudden loss of control can lead to a rash of strange and distorted thinking, odd projections and fears, and an extreme urge to find a reason to run away. But this is what happens when we deal on a reality plane, and a commitment to reality is the only way to get where you're going.

Summary: The New Paradigm

So what does this new paradigm involve? It involves being scared, being willing to give up control, and to recognize that the other person is a real person. It involves doing some work to get to know that person, being willing to get hurt, being open and vulnerable, being honest, and giving up on finding someone who will "save" you. In other words, starting a whole new phase of recovery. It may sound hard, but you can do it. You know this because you have done hard things before.

The rewards of making an effort to try new and frightening behavior and to find ways to hang in there and stay committed to solving problems and being open and levelheaded are great. The new paradigm looks very different from any of the old experiences; it is even different from the "pretty good" old relationships.   In the first line of *Anna Karenina* Tolstoy said "Happy families are all alike." This is true in a way because they all share certain healthy characteristics such as mutual loyalty, respect and support, an atmosphere of easy cooperation and harmony, security, playfulness, and a sense of "oneness." Relationships are supposed to feel good. In Chapter XI we will look in more detail at some of the theories of what healthy relationships all have in common.

VII. Your New Relationship: Eight Dialectical Dilemmas

Parts and wholes evolve in consequence of their relationship, and the relationship itself evolves.

Richard Levins and Richard Lewontin,
The Dialectical Biologist

The next step is to examine some of the basic dilemmas you face as you develop your program for a new and healthier approach to relationships in the future.

As you look over each of these proposed ground rules, you will notice that they all contain a dichotomy and the idea of a *balance between two opposite but valid principles.* As you apply these ideas to yourself and think up your own ground rules, you will often find that there are two seemingly opposing ideas that need to be considered and reconciled into a balanced and evolving approach.

Dialectical thinking is the so-called "middle path." As you no doubt know, addicts are inclined toward thinking in polarities, something is either true or not true, good or bad. But in recovery, rigidity is not your friend. The developmental path you are on will mean giving some energy into thinking through all the facets of an issue, all the changing complexities. When you are stuck, you will need, as Dr. Marsha Linehan has said, "to consider what has been left out or how one has artificially narrowed the boundaries or simplified the problem" (Linehan, 1993). We will talk more about Dr. Linehan and her approach in Chapter X.

1. A healthy relationship style begins with a plan.

Even if you are starting over with the same relationship or marriage that existed pre-recovery, you will want to approach it with new eyes and new ideas as to what you need and how you will behave. It will be harder for some people to start over with the same person because it requires as much (and maybe more) effort to look honestly at an old relationship as it does to evaluate a new one.

When recovering from sexual addiction you cannot just assume that you know how to go about the dating process in a normal way. In fact, you may never have approached the possibility of dating in a way that was not somehow distorted by your addiction. *When you begin dating in recovery, you must be especially conscious of what you are doing.* I knew a woman in recovery who had an addictive compulsion to act out bondage scenarios which included being strangled. She told me laughingly that, in early recovery, she thought she could find a normal relationship and then act out her bondage scenarios within that relationship.

Even if you are very strong in your recovery, you must be aware that your addiction can seep into your relating in ways you are not aware of. That is why you need to be vigilant as you proceed. *The planning exercises* provided in Chapter VIII will help you to be specific and clear about your own basic boundaries and perceptions regarding any particular person or potential relationship. It is very easy to slip into a relationship that seems "totally different" from your usual relationship scenario only to find that it has some key elements in common with your old style. At which point we say "How did that happen?"

The Dilemma

The other side of this dilemma is the basic (and true) recovery idea of trusting your intuition. Sometimes people even consider their intuition as their Higher Power guiding them. Certainly the goal of trusting your intuition is an important one, but which intuition is the right one!? Sometimes your intuition seems to be saying two different things and often the softer voice is the new voice in your head, the voice of awareness that you need to pay attention to. Sometimes talking to a trusted friend in recovery will help you keep perspective on this issue.

I have also found a useful analogy in Chinese nutritional medicine. The idea is that when we are healthy we crave what is good for us or what our bodies need at the time, and that when we are unhealthy we crave the very things that are bad for us and will make us sicker. So as you get healthier in recovery you will be better able to trust that your primary "intuition" is more likely to be correct. Listen to your instincts, but stay vigilant for your "addict's" voice in your head, especially at first.

2. Keep a long focus.

Addictive relationships are formed, and continue, without much in the way of a long-term goal. The addict often wants immediate gratification and, in his or her addictive delusional state, will feel that things should be just right immediately. Sometimes things *are* just right immediately, but that has nothing to do with having a viable relationship. In recovery, potential relationships need to be viewed with the goal of establishing a trusting, loving bond that can be sustained over time. To do so both partners must help each other to remember to be patient and remember that building a relationship is a process. It does not hurt to view the relationship as one would view a developing child, being gentle and allowing for the feelings that develop to go through many phases and overcoming many irrational fears before becoming strong and trustworthy.

The Dilemma

Sometimes people in recovery who are dating will be torn between having a long-term goal for the relationship and taking it *"one day at a time."* Shouldn't we be living "in the moment," not having a bunch of heavy duty expectations to distort our experience? Well this is certainly a valid point, but too often the "one day at a time" idea is used to dodge the fact that addicts need to think about what they are doing in a more careful way. I find that the *lack of intent*, the inability of people to openly talk about their relationship history and what they are looking for in the future is a way of ensuring that the relationship will be limited, a way of ensuring that there is an *exit route*. It is the old fear of intimacy running the show. Remember that in relationship recovery you have the potential to be intimate and safe at the same time!

You will not be "trapped" by your own or any one else's agenda as long as you are able to be open and honest with yourself about how the relationship is progressing. The danger for addicts in recovery is far more in the direction of having no agenda, no idea of a goal and no ability to build something lasting and good.

3. Keep your new relationship in a social context.

Relationships exist and flourish only in a social context. For recovering addicts there is a great temptation to isolate themselves with the person they are dating. Almost as soon as you are "seeing" someone you should plan to get together with each other's best friends and allow yourself to be seen together as a couple. This does not mean that you are going to allow your friends to dictate how your relationship life proceeds. It just means that you will have to be aware of the need to exist in a social context as part of what makes a relationship real. If you are "holed up" as a couple there is a lack of substance and reality to the relationship. We are social creatures, and as a recovering addict you are going to be practicing becoming more comfortable in a social world, whatever it is. After a point you should also make sure to meet each other's significant family members if feasible. And if you have reached a point of sharing your recovery information then it may be a good idea to have coffee or lunch as a couple with your sponsor, or go to a social gathering that includes your recovering friends.

Some social circles will be more comfortable than others, but if you are to have a sense of the reality of your relationship, you will need to practice appearing at social gatherings with people who knew you before you were dating that person. You will no doubt get feedback about the person you showed up with, and that is a good thing. As with all feedback you will have learned in recovery to "take what you liked and leave the rest." But by showing up with someone you will have proved to your friends, your date and most of all to yourself that you have nothing to be afraid of.

The Dilemma

If you are seriously interested in following up with a new relationship, you will undoubtedly feel that it is important to learn as much about each other as you can and experience as many things together, just the two of you, as possible so that you can see whether you are going to be able to build a close and serious bond as a couple. You will certainly want to have a lot of time alone with each other; it's just that having your love relationship in one sector of your life and having everything else you do in another sector of your life is a throwback to the old addictive patterns of shame, fear, and compartmentalization. Like everything in this set of dilemmas it is a matter of striking a balance.

4. No two people get into recovery at the same time.

You may feel that the person you are dating or having a relationship with is more mentally together than you are.

Or you may feel that you are further along in your recovery than the other person. Or you may feel both those things at different times. The fact is different people will always be at different places in various parts of their journey. One person may have more years in recovery but the other person may have developed more of a spiritual awareness or practice. One may be better at compromise and cooperation but the other may be better at confronting issues honestly as they come up. It will be vital that you accept your partner wherever they are. If they were not sincere in their desire to learn and grow in their own way you would not have been willing to be in the relationship.

The Dilemma

It is true that people only have a shot at a healthy relationship if they have about the *same level of emotional maturity* (give or take). This is a reality of relationships. It is not a requirement that we go in with. All along we attract, and are attracted to, people who are at our level of functioning or at our level of emotional maturity. You are probably going to lose interest in someone if you feel they are not able to function and interact with the level of self-awareness and honesty that you have been able to achieve—if they play games, manipulate, are dishonest, or are incapable of being responsible. By the same token, you will likely run away from a potential partner if you feel that compared to you they are functioning at a much higher level: if they are scrupulously honest, high achievers, completely emotionally stable and able to cope with anything, ambitious, highly confident, etc. These are all great attributes, but if you see yourself as struggling with things that are easy for your partner, if you are just beginning to function at your potential and beginning to have the kind of confidence that you need, then the other person may seem to place on you a demand for a level of emotional development that is overwhelming and frightening.

But given that you and your potential partner are in the same ballpark in terms of your growth and level of functioning, it is important to remember that everyone is on their own path, and we cannot expect total synchronicity. Having faith in yourself and having faith in your partner means that while you may be aware of ways in which one of you is struggling more in certain areas, you also have the belief that each of you will find your way. Expecting you and your partner to know the same things and have exactly the same intimacy and relationship skills is unrealistic. Even if it were possible, it would prevent you from having the very important and intimate experience of learning from one another.

5. Be aware of creeping codependency.

Most addicts are also codependents. The Codependents Anonymous "big book" has a great story which describes *codependency as the roots of a tree, and the various addictions as the branches of the tree* (Codependent's Anonymous, 1995). In Chapter V we considered the origins of the addict's problems with relating and the roots of the problem of codependency in terms of childhood messages that convey the idea that my worth as a person is defined by my worth to someone else. Addicts are always prone to revert to *focusing on the other person.*

I believe all recovering sex addicts should familiarize themselves with their own symptoms of codependency rather than simply seeing it as a problem of spouses and partners of addicts. You should consider reading some of the work of Pia Mellody, one of the most important theorists in this field, such as her book *Facing Codependence* (1995). In that book Mellody describes the "five core symptoms of codependence," which are

- Low self-esteem,
- Difficulty setting functional boundaries,
- Difficulty owning our own reality,
- Difficulty acknowledging and meeting our own needs and wants, and
- Difficulty experiencing and expressing our reality moderately.

The symptoms of codependency can take many forms which distort your relationships with others, especially partners and lovers. Often in relationships codependency takes the form of falling into the trap of trying to "help" the other person, help them to be more or like you need them to be, or simply not having a clear enough awareness of their or your own boundaries. A friend of mine who is a recovering codependent has a knack for funny sayings about these issues. One of my favorites is, *"Well it walks like a duck, and it quacks like a duck, but I think I can fix it!"*

Most addicts have had childhood experiences that invalidated them in one way or another and led to their needing, as children, to try endlessly to please a caregiver in the hope that it would lead to being loved and valued. *Therefore, addicts have a deeply ingrained* *tendency to worry about someone else, a need to take care of someone else's needs, to emotionally regulate someone else (e.g. a parent) as a way to gain acceptance and approval. This habit dies hard, and it only decreases as we become able to feel that we are lovable and loved for <u>ourselves.</u>*

The Dilemma

Does this mean that we don't confront things that concern us about the person or the relationship? No, because we will be attempting to practice our new intimacy skills of speaking our truth in the moment and not sweeping things under the rug. But in so doing we will be being careful to talk about ourselves, what we experience and what feelings are aroused in us as objectively as we can. We will take time to think through whether we are trying to make our world more comfortable by changing someone else or whether we are honestly talking about our own process.

Also we will be practicing our relationship skill of listening really, really hard to the other person when we talk about what we think is going on and not just trying to make them see things our way. A mentor of mine says, *"Really listening is like dying for a minute."* This is especially true for those addicts who are most co-dependent in that letting someone in this way may be experienced as extreme vulnerability if a person still lacks confidence that they can set appropriate boundaries so as to protect a new and still fragile sense of self. So you need to be prepared to let go of the impulse to control and maneuver the other person into what you think is right, especially when it comes to their well-being.

A recovery slogan that applies to this situation of needing to let go of control of another person, *to let them do things their way*, is "*How important is it?*" I have found myself on the point of trying to force my husband to use the "right" salad bowl for the salad he was making. Why? He's him and I'm me. He has his own opinion of the "right" salad bowl. What difference does it really make? If this kind of thing is a serious hurdle for you, and it is for many people in recovery, then participating in a 12-Step program for codependency such as Al-Anon is a necessary support. Many sex addicts participate in one or more additional programs and particularly in a program such as Al-Anon.

6. You cannot always be an open book.

I have found that many recovering sex addicts seem to feel so much guilt and remorse about the "wreckage of their past" that they feel they must be honest about absolutely everything all the time. Now while I agree that a healthy relationship will be built on a commitment to honesty and to not keeping secrets, I also feel that addicts sometimes end up going off the deep end. One addict I know tells his wife everything, but he goes way beyond total honesty. He tells her his dreams, well that's OK, and he tells her any fantasies he has, and he forbids himself to have any fantasies or dreams involving sexual attraction to anyone but her. He tries to control not just his fantasies but his dreams! When he can't he feels a need to confess.

The Dilemma

A relationship should be built on trust and honesty. But at the same time we admonish couples to maintain a *separate identity* and not lose their individuality and separate life. In my opinion, everyone needs to have a right to privacy and to their own separate inner life. I feel that this is where a lot of our creativity comes from. However, it is only through a commitment to *rigorous honesty* between people that a level of trust will be established such that each person can be allowed their separate life without it becoming a threat to the bond. I have heard it said that as couples we must be the "guardians of each others' privacy." Ideally the relationship bond will be such that we do not need to know everything that our partner thinks or dreams of. We will come to see our partner's private thoughts as precious and as their own.

7. It is OK to have bad sex.

Being able to have good sex with your partner is important, of course, but it bears repeating that your sexual experience with your partner does not have to be perfect (however you define perfect) every time. Sex addicts in my experience have habitually placed so much emphasis on the sex act being up to a certain level of ecstatic satisfaction that it is hard for them to put it in a proper perspective in their relationship. In this process the couple's sexual relationship takes precedence over the rest of their relationship and in effect becomes alienated from and in a way separate from their intimate life together.

By "bad" sex I certainly do not mean unpleasant, hurtful or unwelcome experiences. I mean only experiences that do not fit a preconceived idea of what is supposed to happen. Having a set idea about what the sexual contact should be like between two people harkens back to the addict's attitude toward his or her addictive acting out behavior. I have an addict friend who summed this up nicely by saying that "In addictive acting out you always know what's going to happen, it's always the same." In this sense addictive sex is boring in its lack of surprises. In an intimate relationship with a partner, sex can take many forms and many moods. The important thing will be to see it as a way of connecting rather than a way to achieve a perfect climax.

The only rule I think is important is that the sexual experience respect the feelings and needs of both people. Not that those needs will be met perfectly every time, but that each partner approaches the experience with caring and generosity as an underlying value.

The Dilemma

Good sex is important too. Many recovering sex addicts will try to bring aspects of their old addictive behaviors and fantasies into the sex act with their partner. I have heard different and seemingly valid attitudes about this issue from different people. Some would say that addictive ideas and fantasies, even "objectifying" one's partner can be present in healthy sex as part of the "*fuel mix.*" Others see this as a slippery slope and would rather force themselves to banish any thoughts or fantasies that hark back to their old "unhealthy" sexual behaviors. I have not formed a strong opinion either way. Once again I feel there is a balance that needs to be struck such that you can experience your sexual fantasies in a way that enhances a healthy experience while avoiding getting stuck in an old addictive pattern that fetishizes your partner and yourself.

Remember that as a recovering sex addict or partner of one, sex is an area where you need to be especially patient and gentle with yourselves. Putting sex and loving intimacy together may be an ongoing challenge.

8. Being OK No Matter What Happens.

Sex addicts are prone to "black and white thinking," also known as "all-or-nothing thinking." Recovering addicts tend to take this mentality into their new relationships. This means that when there is a conflict with someone you are dating, or an aspect of a relationship that reflects your partner's unresolved problems (or your own), it suddenly seems like the relationship is doomed. If her family seems cold toward you, if you feel he is not able to relate to your career interests, if she is too busy, if he still seems to look at other women, etc., then the first impulse may be to flee.

It is important to remember that addicts *do not really believe in intimate relationships.* They have developed a style of relating that over time has kept them *out* of healthy relationships, and part of that style is usually to see minor bumps in the road as disasters! This is where people in recovery already have a set of skills that can see them through, *if they only remember to use them.* This will be the time for *letting go of outcomes.*

If you cannot calm yourself down about whatever you see as the latest disaster, you will not be in a position to deal with it in a healthy way and to take the long view that things will be resolved in time. Use your *spiritual skills* to calm your fears. Tell yourself "We can get through this" even if you don't exactly know how. Remember that you have already learned to have faith that *"This too shall pass."*

Being willing to stay calm and see if things will work out over time does not mean that you accept a situation that is ultimately not right for you. It just means that you give it a chance and don't see every problem or conflict as a "deal breaker." At the same time, to be able to function in a relationship in a mature way you must be able to accept the risk that asserting your feelings and needs may mean the end of the relationship.

The Dilemma

Working on a relationship is a good thing, but being OK without a relationship means that you will not expect yourself to work endlessly to make something work out. Sex addicts in recovery find a lot of support from Recovering Couples Anonymous or from couple therapy or workshops. But ultimately a relationship or marriage is not working if all you do is work on it. Terrence T. Gorski (1993) said it best:

> A healthy person isn't very interested in a relationship that's going to take a lot of work. Healthy people expect the norm of the relationship to be voluntary, free-flowing cooperation. It's comfortable, secure, and it feels nice.

The diagram below summarizes the Eight Dilemmas described in this chapter:

Healthy Relationship Guidelines:
Eight Dialectical Dilemmas

On the One Hand . . .	On the Other Hand . . .
Don't trust your first impressions.	Learn to listen to your intuition.
Be present in the moment; be spontaneous.	Focus on the long-term goal of a solid relationship.
Build a close and loyal bond, a "oneness."	Don't isolate yourself in the relationship.
Partners must be equal in emotional maturity.	No two people are at the exact same place in their journey.
Don't try to "fix" your partner's problems.	Be willing to confront issues between you.
Be honest: Tell it all, tell it soon.	Allow each other to have privacy and a separate "inner life."
Having good sex with your partner is important.	Put sex in a relational context: It's only part of the picture.
Be committed, prepared to hang in there and ride out the rough spots.	Be able to end a relationship and be OK being alone.

VIII. Turning Insight Into Action: Tools for Planning Your Relationship Program

We make a path by walking on it.

Chuang Tzu

New Relationships vs. Recycling Old Relationships

In this section we will look at some tools to help you reach the new relationship style or paradigm. Although these exercises appear to address the addict who is looking for a new partner, you can adapt these exercises to your situation if you have a former spouse or partner and are looking to restart a preexisting relationship on a healthier footing.

As stated previously, I believe that resuming a relationship that existed prior to the addict's disclosure and treatment should involve a process of self-exploration and planning as though it were a new relationship. In the second section below that deals with sober dating, the addict who wishes to get back together with a former partner will have to look at that partner as though they were someone new and decide whether they represent a choice of partner which is based on a new model of relationship recovery or whether there are serious enough problems inherent in the situation with that partner that they are not a realistic candidate for a healthy relationship going forward.

I believe that if you are in this situation and you are honest with yourself, you will have to admit that there were aspects of your prior partner choice that were less healthy for your partner and yourself and were more suited to you as an addict than to you as an addict in recovery. Hopefully your former partner has also been examining their own relationship issues and has made enough progress so that they can play a new and different role in your life and in the relationship, one that works for your new paradigm and your new expectations. This should become clearer as you complete the exercises below.

Self-Worth and the Fear of Dating

Prior to entering recovery, sex addicts who are looking for a potential partner tend to aim either too low or too high. On the one hand, they gravitate toward people whom they perceive as *less* desirable than those they are most drawn to, and therefore "safer." This would include people they see as lesser in some attribute: less attractive, less emotionally mature, less intelligent, or less socially desirable than they are. This is a way of avoiding the rejection they believe would be inevitable were they to go after what they really wanted in a partner. Or, on the other hand, sex addicts gravitate toward people whom they see as highly desirable but, who for one reason or another, really are unavailable. This includes people who are already married, obviously wrong in age or in other socio-cultural factors, or of the wrong sexual orientation. In this case they quickly decide that it is hopeless and withdraw into fantasy about the person which is, also, "safer."

It will be important for any addict in recovery to look at this old relationship pattern as they approach a relationship in recovery. Addictive relationship choices are based in the lack of self-worth and the feeling of being inherently unlovable. Targeting potential partners who are perceived as "better than me" or "lesser than me" rises from this feeling of low self-worth and provides a protective cover which keeps the addict from getting hurt. Feeling superior is safe because there is not that much to lose, and/or less chance of losing it. However, the deck is stacked against the relationship succeeding. Feeling inferior is safe because it allows the addict to retreat from reality into fantasy and confirms the feeling that it is impossible to have anything really good.

Both "better than" and "lesser than" are symptoms of the addict's core beliefs and are essentially the same: devaluing myself and devaluing others are two sides of the same coin. This process in turn leads to resentment and isolation, and to a resistance to enter into the dating process at all. Many addicts justify this withdrawal not as fear but as representing the fact that "I am not cut out for relationships and am better off alone." Others feel they are exempt from confronting the challenge of dating and relationships on religious or spiritual grounds. They may argue that they would rather lead a life of spiritual asceticism, or that they have some religious conviction that they cannot have a partner.

If you are an addict in recovery and approaching dating and relationships with trepidation, I would remind you that you have changed a great deal in recovery and that you now have the ability to practice new skills in relating, to ask for what you need, to stick up for yourself when you need to, and to get hurt without feeling it is the end of the world. But these are skills that are new and that need to be practiced in the context of a real relationship with another person. It would be a mistake to disqualify yourself before you even try.

Three Planning Tools

1. Choosing a Worthy Partner and Being a Worthy Partner

If the only viable relationship is a relationship between equals, as described above in Chapter VI, this implies that you bring to the table roughly equivalent attributes to those you are seeking in someone else. Terence Gorski (1993) said it well:

> Healthy people, when they are single, are not psychotically obsessed with finding a partner. They may be obsessed with becoming a person who's worthy to be loved. If you put the same energy in becoming a person who is worthy of love, you don't have to compulsively hunt out somebody to love, someone will find you.

Many sex addicts who are in good recovery have some idea of what they would like their future partner to be like, but often they lack a realistic view of themselves. As an addict in recovery you may still see the relationship world in a lopsided way. You may be overly focused on the other person, obsessed with what the other person has to offer you and oblivious of what you have to offer them, or what you *don't* have to offer them! The radical change involved in learning a new way of relating, a new way of looking at potential partners and, in general, a new "relationship style" is that it will begin with a realistic appraisal of yourself and a plan to change those areas that need changing. By the way, this level of change is involved in all your relationships, your friendships, your family relationships, etc. How good a partner, lover, friend, or relative are you?

You may think that becoming a person worthy of love (or friendship) is an enormous undertaking, but you will be surprised at how easy it really is. You don't have to change your personality or your essential nature. You can still be the "real" you, recognizable to yourself and others. It is that you will have made a decision to take *actions*, sometimes big action, sometimes very small actions, that honor your life and honor the relationships that grace your life.

You might start with making a list of the (1) qualities that describe people and (2) those that are important to you about someone else. Using the spaces below, list *ten categories* or life domains with which you would describe a person. You can make up your own, or you can use the examples suggested here. Then specify what you would want that person to be like in terms of that dimension.

Ten Life and Personal Domains

Examples: looks, level of education, capacity for devotion, physical activity, interests, intellectuality, personality type, emotional maturity, family situation (children, etc.), spirituality/religion, level of accomplishment, sophistication in a particular area (specify).

1. _____
2. _____
3. _____
4. _____
5. _____
6. _____
7. _____
8. _____
9. _____
10. _____

Qualities You Would Value in a Partner

For each of the ten areas above describe what you would most value in someone who might be a partner for you.

Examples: healthy good looks, training or experience in something they care about, able to fully commit, some athletic interests, sociable but also introspective, no children at home, any religion OK, financially stable, competent to solve problems and deal with new situations.

1. _____
2. _____
3. _____
4. _____
5. _____
6. _____
7. _____
8. _____
9. _____
10. _____

Your Self-Rating on the Above 10 Traits

Make a list of 10 of *your own attributes* which specifies how you measure up in each of those specific areas.

Examples: If you would like someone who is "caring and nurturing," then ask yourself are *you* capable of being caring and nurturing? If you would like a partner who is athletic and attractive, ask yourself if *you* are athletic and attractive. If you would like someone who is financially stable ask yourself if *you* are financially stable.

1. _____
2. _____
3. _____
4. _____
5. _____
6. _____
7. _____
8. _____
9. _____
10. _____

Mark those areas where you have noted a difference in what you want and what you have to offer. Take a hard look at your own self-evaluation. Do you have exciting or meaningful work or activities? Have you got too much financial debt? Are you nurturing? Have you put on too many pounds? Do you remember people's birthdays? Do you have a group of interesting friends? If you find that there are areas where you have overlooked your own lack of desirability, then make a commitment to work on those areas. *Make a list of ways in which you could be a better friend, a better lover, and a better partner.*

A simple example is being a better communicator. Let's say you don't remember to keep in touch with people and to make a point of catching up with friends periodically, and you don't initiate getting together with them very often. You don't have to transform yourself into a social butterfly, all you have to do is make a commitment to yourself that you will call certain people and get together with them fairly regularly. This is a change of habit in large part. In addiction, many people have trouble maintaining relationships and communicating regularly because they are alienated from themselves and others and feel "less than." Being a good communicator will be based on your new set of recovery beliefs about yourself. You will now realize that you are a good and decent human being and you deserve to have good friends, but the old habit of not keeping in touch with people still needs to be consciously looked at and consciously changed. Changing an old habit sometimes takes some effort, but it is not mapping the genome. It's just a matter of practice.

Lastly, make a plan to make changes in yourself to better conform with what you believe is good and valuable in a person or a partner. List however many goals you have and commit to making those changes. Be sure that the changes you commit to will be things that enhance your life whether you have a partner or whether you are single. If you work on becoming a person you like then no matter what happens with your "star search" for a partner, you will be making things better and more satisfying for yourself.

Worthy Partner Goals

Examples: I will get a better work situation and get out of debt; I will reconnect with my brother; I will work on paying more attention to my close friendships; I will lose 10 pounds; I will be more flexible.

1. _____
2. _____
3. _____
4. _____
5. _____

Action Plan

For each of the goals you described above, write a set of specific actions you will take to achieve that goal. Try to give at least two or three specific things you can do right away. This may take some thought.

- Goal #1 Action Plan:

- Goal #2 Action Plan:

- Goal #3 Action Plan:

- Goal #4 Action Plan:

- Goal #5 Action Plan:

2.   Make a Sober Dating Plan.

In Chapter III we discussed the reasons why when you start dating in recovery you need to be vigilant as to the people you choose to date and how you go about the dating process. *This process of planning and ongoing evaluation is equally necessary in the situation in which a couple is attempting to reinvent a relationship that existed prior to the disclosure of the addiction.* In either situation, you will be looking at your potential date or partner in a new and more conscious way. You will use your plan to help evaluate the other person, but you will also use the plan to help you look at your own behavior patterns that existed in your old addictive relationship style. These may well include seductiveness, predatory flirting, objectification or any of a large set of behaviors designed to control, avoid or manipulate in lieu of honesty, self awareness and courage.

Even in recovery, you are still going to be susceptible to that peculiar feeling of "instant connection" with someone, that feeling of "familiarity." That feeling should be a warning signal to take stock of the situation and be aware that an instant connectedness may indicate that you have come across someone who fits your past pattern of relationships in which healthy love and commitment are not possible. In other words it may be an illusion.

Many people have questions about *how and when to disclose their sexual history with a person they are dating.* Obviously if the person you go out with is also in sexual recovery then it would be appropriate to share your histories with each other right away. Likewise, it is easier to tell more sooner if the person already knows that you have been receiving treatment for sexual addiction. In this case, the process of eventually disclosing everything and relating in an open way will be accelerated. As to people with no knowledge of your sexual recovery issues, it will be necessary to get yourself to begin to share something about your problem right away. This will not have to be the whole story, but remember, you will be taking the dating process more slowly and carefully than many other people and you will need to let the person know what's going on with you in general so they can make sense out of the experience.

As you get to know someone you are dating, you will have to share more of the "gory details" of your story so that the other person can know the real you; don't forget to include the part about how well you've done in your recovery! If and when you want to be really intimate and committed, you will have to be prepared to share everything—no secrets.   Anything less will sooner or later come home to roost as a <u>betrayal</u>. This is because the other person will feel that regardless of whether things have gone well or badly, they were not able to base their own decisions and behavior on reality. They will likely feel that their reality has been manipulated and will correctly see this as less than caring on your part.

The Sober Dating Plan outline will ask that you put down in some detail your own individualized plan relative to the key questions about dating including some rules about how and when you will let a relationship become sexual. It is important to realize that having sexual feelings for someone you are spending time with, and even having sexual fantasies about them are most likely normal experiences and as such should not cause any alarm.

Problems arise, however, when you allow yourself to believe that your sexual attraction to someone means they are automatically right for you. It takes considerable effort and feedback from trusted advisors to hold on to the reality that you still do not really know a person and that you may not be compatible with them and may not even like them. Until you figure these things out, you may be headed for a casual sexual encounter. This would not be part of the plan for recovering sex addicts. Also you should bear in mind that fantasies are one thing, but if you begin to obsess about or sexually target a person, even someone you know well, this is a definite red flag.

The time to construct a Sober Dating Plan is before you start dating, even before you think you are really ready to start dating. Many addicts in recovery are fearful of dating. They may think they have something to be ashamed of, they may not know how to go about it, and they may have spent years hiding in their addiction. Make a plan and try to stick to it (or modify it if you need to – nothing is perfect.) Remember to check in with others as you go along and listen to their opinions. It's a learning process.

There is no question that as you experiment with dating and relationships in recovery you will make mistakes. This is why the Sober Dating Plan asks you to check in with a therapist, sponsor or other trusted person regularly as your new (or renewed) relationship proceeds. *But if you can take the time to make a serious dating plan (even if you are dating your spouse) and stick to it, you will have gone a long way toward changing your old relationship style and becoming confident with real intimacy.*

Use the outline below to create your own sober dating plan.

Ground Rules about People to Date

Appropriateness of Potential Dates

Suggestions:

- "I will not date anyone I met through any Inner or Middle circle activity."

- "I will not date anyone I met through an online ad that is suspect."

- "I will not date anyone I met when they were dating a friend of mine."

- "I will not date anyone who is more than a few years different from me in age."

- "I will not date anyone where there is a significant power differential."

What are your rules for how you will avoid obviously inappropriate people?

_____

_____

_____

_____

_____

_____

_____

_____

_____

Who are your trusted advisors and how often will
you check in with them?

Suggestions:

- "I will check in with [Names of friends in recovery
  who have experience in sober dating.]"

- "I will have my sponsor meet the person or at least
  check in with my sponsor or trusted persons before
  and after seeing a potential date."

Names of trusted advisors and plan for feedback:

_____

_____

_____

_____

_____

_____

_____

_____

General Rules Once You Have Started Dating

Personalize these rules with notes that apply to you (add
to each as dating progresses):

"I will ask that the person share their relationship history
openly and honestly and will look for problematic patterns."

"I will not continue dating someone who is dating someone else or has recently ended a relationship that may not be completely resolved."

"I will do a 'red-light, yellow-light, green-light' exercise with any dating partner, i.e., 3 lists of attributes specifying positive (green) questionable (yellow) and deal-breaker (red) things I have discovered as I get to know the person. I will add to the lists as I go along and share it with my therapist, sponsor or other trusted advisor."

_____

_____

_____

_____

_____

_____

"I will be particularly alert to whether the person has the capacity to give intimacy, affection and commitment."

_____

_____

_____

_____

_____

_____

_____

_____

"I will be particularly alert as to whether the person is interested in relating in a serious way vs. being just seductive. I will ask *pointed questions* about what the person is looking for and be vigilant for vague answers."

_____

_____

_____

_____

_____

_____

_____

_____

"I will be vigilant about whether I am distorting my view of a person or relationship so as to pursue a sexual obsession."

_____

_____

_____

_____

_____

_____

_____

_____

_____

_____

_____

"I will check in often as to whether the relationship is becoming addictive in any way for me, including whether I am kidding myself about what I feel for them."

_____

_____

_____

_____

_____

_____

_____

_____

_____

_____

_____

Ground Rules for When to Have Sex

How long will you date before agreeing to have sex?

Examples:

- "I will not have sex until I have had a chance to assess the person's character and my own motives."
- "I will not have sex until I have gone on six dates."
- "I will not have sex until I have dated the person for four months."
- "I will not have sex unless we are _____ (committed/engaged/married)."

List your rules for when you will have sex.

1. _____
   _____
2. _____
   _____
3. _____
   _____

What are your bottom line issues?

Examples:

- "I will not have sex with anyone I could not commit to."
- "I will not have cyber sex, sexting, etc."

- "I will not expect to bring my acting-out fantasies into the relationship in any way."

- "I will not have sex with a sex addict who is not in good recovery."

List your rules surrounding sex in recovery:

1. _____

2. _____

3. _____

4. _____

5. _____

Ground Rules for Sharing Your Program Information

These will vary in little ways according to the specific situation, but you should be prepared to:

a. Share early in the dating relationship the fact that you have had sexual and relationship issues in the past and therefore need to proceed slowly.

b. Check in with your sponsor or therapist about how much to share and when before you do it.

c. Before you begin a *sexual* relationship you must share your acting out history in some detail (including your recovery activities) and allow the other person the opportunity to digest this information and decide how they feel.

Internet Dating Services and Social Media

For those who are looking for a new partner, the question arises as to how to go about searching for someone. Compared to the old-fashioned ways of meeting people, i.e., groups around shared interests and activities, career related contacts, being "set up" by friends, answering singles ads or, more recently, "speed dating," the online dating services seem so much more efficient and convenient. Meeting people through the Internet can be very appropriate for some people, if it is done in a careful and appropriate way.

Example from Real Life
A straight sex addict—I'll call him Denny, was interested in finding a new relationship after having been in several years of recovery from addiction to exhibitionism, phone sex and prostitutes. Due to his lack of experience with healthy intimacy and his deep hunger for nurturance, Denny tended to glom onto any woman he dated and get involved too fast. His therapist suggested that Denny go on dates with ten different women before he decide to pursue a relationship with any one woman. This was a clever strategy. It forced Denny to have a variety of experiences and to evaluate them both in terms of how he felt about them and how they responded to him. This gave him a clearer sense of what he was looking for and a better fix on how others perceived him. It also allowed him to slow down and act in a more considered way. Since Denny had no history of being addicted to Internet pornography or cybersex, going online to meet women did not trigger any of his acting out scenarios and so was a safe way to meet a large number of women and try out dating them in a relatively fast and efficient way. Denny fairly quickly found

an appropriate partner—although they met not online, but at a professional conference!

Online dating services are problematic for certain recovering sex addicts because of two aspects of the Internet which may work against the successful formation of relationships. The same problems exist in the use of social media as well.

The first kind of problem arises when the addict has been accustomed to use the Internet as part of their addiction. This would be the case for an addict who had compulsively used the Internet for anonymous sex or "hook-ups," or someone who had used the Internet to meet people in a way that was unrealistic and served their addiction.

Example from Real Life
A straight woman, call her Martha, had a long history of indiscriminate sex, anonymous sex and sadomasochistic relationships with boyfriends. She had used the Internet to find acting out partners prior to getting into recovery. Part of her addictive fantasy was that she would meet the perfect partner who would be rich, handsome, and successful and would meet all of her needs and make her life perfect. Meanwhile, she was a mess and had no hope of actually attracting such a man. In early recovery she decided that she could look for men to date at online dating services. Not only was she totally unable to be realistic about what she thought was the "appropriate" kind of man to date, she tended to accept at face value the most outrageously suspect of the ads she saw, thus setting herself up to meet men who were totally misrepresenting themselves and who might not be safe to meet or go out with. In other words, the Internet was not her friend; it was part and parcel of her

addiction, and she was unable to stay in good contact with reality when using it for dating purposes.

The second circumstance that could make online dating services inappropriate for a particular recovering addict is the fact that *the whole process of advertising online and looking for people to date online can promote fantasy and avoidance.* The recovering addict who is prone to fantasy and prefers to escape from human contact can use dating services to stay entrenched in a pattern of avoidance. A recovering addict who has been addicted to Internet pornography and used the Internet to escape actual contact with real human beings can easily get hooked on browsing the dating sites and compulsively checking for "hits." When it comes time to actually meet, he or she may end up ducking out. A recovering addict whose addictive behavior involved numerous short term serial seductions can use the Internet to date forever, and no one will ever be "good enough." In this case the process of Internet dating makes it possible to avoid finding a person with whom there is a realistic possibility of an intimate connection.

As a recovering addict you will have to evaluate for yourself what the risks and potential benefits of Internet dating and social media connecting are for you. You will have to talk to your sponsor or therapist and make sure you are making a realistic assessment. You should definitely not rule out Internet dating, but if you decide to go that route you should be vigilant to your own process as you proceed.

3. Construct a Relationship "Circle Plan."

A Sober Relationship Circle Plan will be used to describe those behaviors which place a relationship at risk or make it less than healthy (Inner Circle), those behaviors which are "slippery" and might be danger signs (Middle Circle) and those that are good for the relationship and nurture it (Outer Circle). Since you have been in a program for addiction recovery you have undoubtedly come across some version of this formula. It is basically a list of the "dos," the "don'ts," and the "don't even think about its."

The Circle Plan Used in Sex Addiction Treatment

The template for the relationship circle plan is the circle plan commonly used in sex addiction treatment. It is sometimes configured differently, and "Inner Circle behaviors" are sometimes referred to as "bottom line behaviors." But in one form or another it should be familiar to all recovering sex addicts. I have reiterated the general rules used to construct a circle plan in sex addiction treatment below. This will help to give the gist of the task for completing the *relationship circle plan* that follows.

The Inner Circle lists the behaviors that you decide are out of bounds *for you.* For sex addicts these might include any of the following: (1) Your compulsive sexual behaviors such as Internet pornography, cybersex, prostitutes, phone sex, serial seduction/affairs and so on; (2) behaviors which have gotten you in trouble such as exhibitionism, voyeurism or other illegal activities; and (3) behaviors which have been done in secret or violated the trust of another, or which have had negative consequences in your life. In sex addiction recovery your failure to stay away from these behaviors is considered a "slip" or a "relapse."

The Middle Circle contains those behaviors which are deemed "slippery," i.e. those things which might lead you back into your inner circle behaviors such as viewing certain kinds of books, magazines or TV shows, hanging around a certain neighborhood, driving through a certain part of town, etc. Anything that has been associated with the Inner Circle behaviors such as drugs, drinking to excess, gambling, even business trips alone could be classified as Middle Circle depending on the person.

The Outer Circle contains a list of those activities that promote recovery and support a balanced and happy life and lifestyle. These are typically enjoyable activities, activities involving friends and companions, recovery activities such as support group meetings, meaningful work, and activities that support spiritual growth.

A Relationship Recovery Circle Plan

This idea of a Relationship Circle Plan is _not_ intended to be a matter of keeping track of a "sobriety date," as is done in a 12-Step program. It is only intended as a way to think about what things will cause you the most problems and to be aware of the things that may lead to old ways of behaving in relationships. If your old relationship scenario involves avoiding commitments or fleeing from relationships, it may be that your Middle Circle will help you see when you are allowing old fears to overtake you. If your old relationship scenario involved staying in relationships that were beyond repair long after you should have moved on, then your Middle Circle should include ways to make yourself take the needed steps to really be able to end a relationship and not fall back into something that is never going to work or doing an on-again-off-again pattern.

The Relationship Inner Circle lists the elements of your old relationship style which are out of bounds for you. Look back at your Relationship Inventory and your relationship scenario and make a list of specific ways of relating that you need to abstain from because they have the potential to destroy real intimacy. Obviously, your Inner Circle will include behaviors that are attempts to bring your old sexually addictive behaviors into the context of your relationship. This will be a very individual matter for you to judge but it might include such things as trying to get your spouse or partner into three-way sex situations (when that is not their preference) because that was one of your old addictive behaviors or most highly charged addictive fantasies. It might also include using sex to control or manipulate your partner in some way.

Your Inner Circle will also have to include behaviors which are dishonest and disloyal, particularly involving secret or special relationships with others that you know would be seen as a serious betrayal by your partner. Privacy is one thing, compartmentalizing life is something else. You can also include in your Inner Circle ways you typically behaved in the past that you now see had the effect of creating distance between you—such as hiding your true feelings about major areas of life to "placate" your partner. Or you might include manipulations you have typically used in the past such as attempts to "triangulate," i.e. use a third party to create a triangle and thus stir up drama by eliciting jealousy.

Anything that you have tended to become obsessed about in relationships in the past should be considered for possible inclusion in the Inner Circle. This means that if you are becoming obsessed with something you must be committed to *doing something about it* (talking to a trusted person, taking action etc.) rather than just allowing the obsession to grow.

The Relationship Middle Circle will, like the Relationship Inner Circle, include behaviors which are danger signs or behaviors which may lead to slipping back into your old relationship scenarios. These might include ways in which you begin to allow yourself to become competitive or judgmental with your partner rather than staying committed to cooperation. It might also include avoiding trying to "fix" your partner's problems instead of letting them deal with things their way. For some people *sexual avoidance* will be a sign that they are slipping into wanting to move their sex life out of their relationship life.

The Middle Circle is also the place you may want to list the possible risk of *other addictions* emerging. Many people in good recovery from sex addiction need to look out for other addictive behaviors that may crop up around food, work, money, etc.

Social avoidance, finding yourself isolated *in* your relationship may also be one of your problem tendencies. It may help you to review the Eight Dilemmas chart in Chapter VII for ideas about what things might apply to your Middle Circle.

The Outer Relationship Circle is where you describe your new relationship style, your new paradigm. You may include new behaviors to practice which involve letting go of control and trusting your partner more. It may also include practicing cooperative behaviors, helping and supporting your partner, and remembering to demonstrate that you are positive and proud of your partner and your relationship.

You might include in your Relationship Outer Circle making time for things that support your relationship, but that tend to get lost in the shuffle, such as taking trips together (or separately), making sure you have time for sex and non-sexual physical intimacy, and working on your own program of recovery.

You may feel that you and your partner do not share the exact same spiritual level of awareness. This is not a problem, as we will see in Chapter X, as long as you consciously seek out the areas in which you can learn from your partner's spirituality, even if it takes a different form than your own. Think about what your partner does that is most fulfilling to them, then try to understand and identify with that in yourself.

Sample Plan

Below is one sample Circle Plan for a fictional person in relationship recovery. It is only one hypothetical person's plan and should not be used as a guide for you. You will come up with your own plan that is specifically geared toward you and your current or potential partner.

If you are honest with yourself, you will find over time that there are things you forgot to include and new things that become more important to add. *You can change the plan as you go along,* referring back to your overall goals for a new relationship style that is one of cooperation, mutual support, availability, vulnerability, honesty and fun.

As you will see in the next chapter, the tools for trans-
forming your relationship style that are discussed in this
chapter are only a beginning. In the following chapters
you will see other ways to use the recovery skills that are
already familiar to you and to build on them as you build a
new relationship.

Sample Circle Plan for Relationship Recovery

OUTER
- Compliment my partner often.
- Build in time to enjoy nature together.
- Be the guardian of my partner's privacy.
- Support my partner's interests and be willing to learn from him/her.
- Cultivate good friends as a couple.
- Create sensual time together, trading massages, etc.
- Plan time for sex.

MIDDLE
- Unnecessary business travel, especially to places with casinos.
- Needing to drink alcohol before we have sex.
- Criticizing my partner's adherence to his/her recovery program.
- Being demanding and negative.
- Too much sarcasm directed at my partner.

INNER
- Emailing old girlfriends or old acting out partners.
- Becoming obsessed with or flirting with a friend or someone at work.
- Insisting that we watch porn.
- Comparing my partner to others unfavorably.
- Making covert threats of abandonment.

Relationship Circle Plan

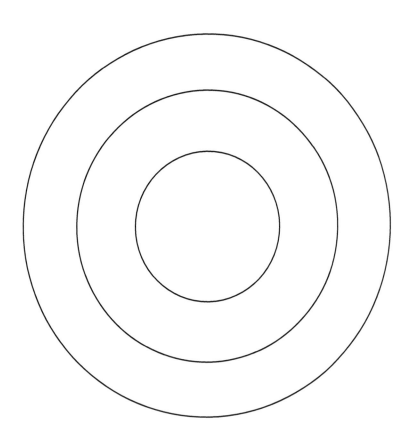

The Unintended Consequences of Change

The act of doing something differently than you have ever done it before—the act of breaking an old pattern of defenses—can be experienced as roughly analogous to throwing a brick through a jewelry store window. *Self-activating* in a way that allows you to change direction is no small undertaking; it is taking the reins in your own life. Instead of reacting to things based upon old unconscious patterns laid down decades ago, you are cutting the ties that bind you to those old patterns and old defensive ways of behaving.

You are no doubt familiar with the idea that when you change, those around you may not like it. Even if you change for the better, and even if you change the way they want you to change, you are breaking the old rules about who they thought you were. They may feel abandoned and like they no longer know you. As you also know, they will have to adapt to a healthier you, (and probably get healthier themselves in the process) or they will have to leave the relationship.

What may be an unfamiliar reality is that taking the reins in your life in general, and in your relationship life in particular, and operating in a healthier, more proactive way will often leave *you* with a feeling of emotional let-down and loss. What is the loss? It is the loss of an imaginary bond with a parent or caregiver based on re-enacting some behavioral adaptation that you believed in your child's mind could bring forth the love you needed. It is the letting go of the fantasy of the "good" part of the parent-child relationship that was never there. Dr. James Masterson (1985) describes this process in his writing in terms of a cycle in which self-activation (breaking old patterns) leads to feelings of depression which can lead to resuming old roles which do not work, and then deciding to self-activate again. If taking action in a different way, being more assertive and clear with people makes you feel strangely lonely, you can very likely see this as a byproduct of something good; it can be one indicator of behaving in a healthier way.

When we let go of old defenses and become less egotistical, we are letting go of a piece of old baggage. As we become more proactive, we may be perceived by others as less reactive and it may seem to them, and even to us, that something is missing. In reality we are not letting go of any important part of our personality; we are still who we are, only stronger, more individuated and more effective.

IX. Using Basic Recovery Skills to Deal with 10 Common Relationship Challenges

To field a ground ball must be considered a generous act and an act of comprehension. One moves not against the ball but with it. Bad fielders stab at the ball like an enemy. This is antagonism. The true fielder lets the path of the ball become his own path, thereby comprehending the ball and dissipating the self, which is the source of all suffering and poor defense.

Chad Harbach, *The Art of Fielding*

Most of the tools and skills you already learned to help you in your recovery from your addiction can be adapted in one form or another to deal with the day-to-day challenges that arise as you confront relationships in recovery. Some of these are:

1. *Internal* processes of learning to redirect your thinking, letting go of harmful emotions and attitudes, and reciting recovery mantras to help you focus on what is really important. Other internal recovery skills are those of maintaining a level of rigorous honesty, noticing and reflecting on your own internal emotional states, and learning to stay "present" in the moment and attend to one thing at a time.

2. *External* skills such as *reaching out* to trusted people to give you advice or perspective, talking to a therapist or sponsor, and going to support groups.

3. *Planning and prevention* exercises involve such things as anticipating your Relapse Scenario, the clear awareness on your part of what could set the stage for a relapse and maintaining lifestyle balance, i.e., learning how to recognize the signs of stress or poor self-care in various aspects of daily life.

4. *Spiritual tools* develop the ability to tap into the peace, serenity and sense of connectedness that recovery inevitably brings. In Chapter XII, "Relationships as Spiritual Practice," we will talk about the spiritual dimension of relationships.

Examples of Relationship Challenges

Here are some ideas for using these basic recovery skills as you navigate dating and relationship experiences in recovery. Some of these are *skills that take practice* and some are more like *slogans or mantras* that you can reach for when you feel angry, frightened, or confused. You know what works best for you, and you will undoubtedly think of other things you learned in your recovery and other insights that you had that you can adapt to these new situations.

In what follows I will go through some typical challenging experiences that people talk about when pursuing a relationship in recovery or beginning an old relationship anew in recovery. I will give examples starting from the first intimacy challenges that may arise in the beginning of a dating situation, later intimacy obstacles that arise as you pursue a relationship and situations that challenge the integrity of a relationship after it has been established.

These are *only examples* and are not meant to be an exhaustive list of all possible challenges that may arise. Also, they are general situations that will be experienced differently by different people, and I know you will encounter your own particular situations as you proceed. I only hope you will refer to these examples as they apply to you along the way and that you will realize two things:

- <u>That these challenges are to be expected</u> when a person in recovery tries their wings in a romantic relationship, and

- <u>That you already have many of the basic skills</u> to succeed if you only adapt them to the task of developing a new relationship style and becoming intimacy literate.

As you read about these challenges, you may get more ideas about things that you want to consider in your relationship recovery plan or things you may want to go back and add to your Relationship Recovery Circle plan.

1. The "Not Right Person Challenge"

This is often the first challenge that can block even the attempt at relationships entirely. I like to think of it as the *myth of the "not-right-person."* This is an avoidance mechanism that comes from an old pattern of wanting to dodge any relationship that doesn't work perfectly for you. Feeling cut off and/or ignorant about relationships in the past you may have operated on the assumption that a suitable partner would be someone who would be a perfect match for you and would make everything OK.

This actually may have served some people's addictive relationship style quite well, keeping them away from any kind of genuine connection and commitment and protecting them from what might be felt as intolerable demands. But mostly it makes the whole endeavor *about the other person and not about the act of building something together.*

There are a number of recovery ideas and mantras to grab hold of when you find yourself dismissing someone because they are not _____ [you fill in the blank]. You already have the recovery concept of *accepting people where they are* and *"not taking someone else's inventory."* One of the Al-Anon slogans is "keep an open mind." You would be surprised how hard this is for some people. A bright, attractive 40-something woman therapist I know requires that a man she dates must be in the therapy profession (among other things). Unsurprisingly, she has been single all her life. A man I know in recovery ended a perfectly good relationship simply because his girlfriend was of a different spiritual persuasion. If he had *reached out to trusted recovery friends and listened to them* he might have been able to get past this (or at least practice some relationship skills) but instead he bolted, returning to sexual acting out.

Bottom line, a relationship may not work out even if you give it a chance, but it should be because you really aren't compatible and not because you have peremptorily written the other person off.

2. The "Dating That Goes Nowhere" Challenge

There are a number of things that could be going on here, but one of the most important is that you may not be being "rigorously honest" about what it is you are doing and what you want. You already have the basic recovery skill of looking at yourself, of taking your own inventory and examining your own behavior.

A gay man I know who is in good recovery has started to get his feet wet with dating. He mentioned a new man whom he liked and who seemed quite interested in him. They spent some time together, and then nothing happened. I asked what happened, and he told me the guy hadn't called him. I asked why he hadn't called the guy and taken the initiative himself. This was something he had never thought of doing!

This goes back to the addictive relationship style of avoiding being clear about what it is you are looking for. There may be many reasons for this, including residual ambivalence and/or anger at potential partners, or an old style of objectifying people and having fleeting seductions. If this challenge keeps happening to you it will be necessary to take your own inventory, consult with a trusted person, and *practice* being clear about what you want in a relationship. You will also have to practice telling a potential partner what your intentions are and being able to do so fairly early on in a dating relationship. Surprisingly, it won't make the other person feel "pressured," but it may result in you getting the information you need (and may not want) about *their* intentions and wishes.

3. The "Irrational Fears" Challenge

Early on in a relationship or dating situation it is normal to feel freaked out and a little crazy. If you are a recovering addict, this is uncharted territory and your mind may make up all kinds of stories about what is going on with the other person. Are they who they say they are? Are they about to dump me? etc., etc. In your addictive style of interacting you were much more in control, or thought you were. In recovery, a new relationship is an experiment in terror. Nothing is as familiar, safe and predictable as it was before. This can result in a kind of delusional thinking designed to make some familiar sense out of the unknown and unpredictable.

Your self-soothing recovery skills come in handy here, as well as your ability to check in with someone for a reality check. If you have learned to keep a journal, that is to write down what is going on, you will find it a good way to allow yourself time to look at your thoughts and feelings and gain perspective. The recovery notions of "one day at a time" and "letting go of outcomes" are particularly useful here. Perhaps your worst fears will come true (probably not), but it is helpful to remember the importance and the effectiveness of not having any expectations. Wishes sure, but let go of any hope of feeling control over anybody else or anything outside of yourself. Leave the outcomes in the hands of your Higher Power.

4. The "Loss of Self" Challenge

One of the most common experiences in early relationship recovery is the deep and primitive fear of *loss of identity, of losing yourself in another person.* Most often it is an irrational fear that you will turn to mush and be under the other person's control. Sometimes it takes the form of the reciprocal fear of being abandoned: If I lose this partner, I will die; I will cease to exist. Either way, fear of abandonment or fear of engulfment, can cause behavior that is distancing or clinging and which causes the relationship to falter. This is a good time to talk to a therapist, sponsor or trusted friend. Journaling may serve to help you in this period too by allowing you to talk about your irrational thought process and get some distance from it.

These fears of loss of self exist because your new self, your recovery self, is still developing strength. Your new self is not yet entirely sure that it can keep its balance and protect you. This will be familiar to you as the recovery issue of "boundaries." Boundaries are behaviors by which you take care of yourself. Your newly formed ability to set boundaries, decide what works for you and act on it, is what gives you strength in the conviction that you can protect this "self" and that there is no danger from without that you cannot deal with. Boundaries allow you to be safe and to let go of the fear of losing your "self." In this way you take control of your life. You can protect your identity and get your needs met yourself regardless of what your partner is doing or not doing.

Using these and other tools of recovery will enable you to get through this difficult phase of a relationship in recovery and, best case, if the relationship works out, you will look back and laugh at how crazy you felt in the beginning.

5. The "Victim Role" Challenge

This is a situation in which the recovering addict reverts to his or her old relationship style of feeling dominated or downtrodden by their partner. One common way this is experienced is when the recovering addict in a relationship sees himself as *"in the dog house,"* needing to prove to the partner that he can be counted on to be honest and trustworthy.

This goes awry when the need to rebuild trust is interpreted as a need to be compliant with what your partner wants and demands at all times. This can lead right back into a "roller coaster" addictive relationship style where things are great when you are a "good" boy/girl and things are combative and punitive when you do something "wrong." In either situation, the recovering addict is dealing with a situation which is a set-up for resentment. In their past addictive relationships, such addicts would use the resentment about feeling "victimized" and "self-sacrificing" as an excuse to compensate themselves by an episode of sexual acting out. The addict would feel inadequate and disadvantaged in the relationship and feel he deserved the "reward" of his sexually addictive behavior which would only add to his feelings of shame and inferiority to his partner.

Regardless of what your partner's problems may be, whether they are used to having a "damaged" partner and fall into the role of disciplinarian, or whether they are angry because of years of trauma, betrayal and deception or both, your job as the addict attempting to have a healthy relationship is to learn to be more assertive than you have ever been before about what you are feeling and what you need. Anything less is "projecting" onto the other person what is your own responsibility.

The recovery saying that works here is "You always have choices." If you feel that the demands on you are too great, you have the choice to speak up, set boundaries, and make sure you create a life that will work for you. A therapist or counselor may be a necessary support, not for you as a couple but for you the addict as an individual. This is one of those times, as Patrick Carnes has said, to "come to your own assistance." *This also means being willing to ask for what you need,* not expecting that if you make the partner happy everything will be great. It also means being able to carve out time to continue your work on your own recovery.

Many addicts lack very basic assertiveness skills, and these need to be practiced, even if imperfectly at first, in order to make the relationship possible. Addicts come from shame, and that shame has not been completely expunged for most recovering addicts as they approach relationships. As Jonathan Young, the Director of the Center for Story and Symbol, has said in his lectures, *"Shame does not speak up."*

6. The "Comfort Zone" Challenge

As you begin relationships in recovery, you will be radically changing from your old relationship style to a new one. You will be doing a lot of things you never did before and behaving in new and different ways. These will be things that are in the Outer Circle of your Relationship Recovery Circle plan. Perhaps you are not used to talking so much about your feelings or about what is going on between you. You may find it hard to adopt a new attitude of being open and vulnerable. You may find that it is scary to tell the person you are dating that you don't want to see them tonight because you need some time to yourself. You may find that you want to do things together such as go to events, socialize with family and friends that are not always easy. Sometimes you may feel you are playing a role that is unfamiliar. *All in all there may be many situations in which you will find yourself out of your comfort zone!*

This is a good time to go back to your addictive Relationship Inventory from Chapter IV and notice what things you are attempting to change. Remember that in recovery there is always talk about "new behavior" and how scary and exciting that can and should be. You have already practiced this concept in your own recovery so far: being honest when you would have lied, reaching out to others for help when you would have holed up in the past. You need to remind yourself that you already know how to do new behavior and *you already know how to do hard things.*

The fact is that as you evolve in your recovery you will probably be doing everything differently than you did before to a greater or lesser degree and it is this new way of conducting your life, this willingness to go *outside of your comfort zone* that is going to continue to allow you to reap the "fruits of recovery," especially in the relationship domain.

One of the major areas in which addicts will be challenged to behave differently is in the area of *cooperation*. The new relationship paradigm requires you to let go of any old model of intimate relating built on competition and manipulation. This can be very frightening. Suddenly there's another person there who may or may not agree with what you want. There is another recovery slogan that you can reach for in this situation: "Live and let live."

The reciprocal of letting the other person be or feel differently is that it's OK for you to disagree. As we discussed in the preceding section, it may be a new and sometimes uncomfortable behavior to do something *you* want to do. A wise woman in Al-Anon once said: "It's OK to do something somebody else doesn't like."

7. The "Terrible Twos" Challenge

This seems to be a phase in relationships that is common to people whether or not they are addicts in recovery. Developing relationships have been likened to developing children, going through an infancy phase characterized by fusion or dependence followed by an individuation phase in which the two partners realize that they are separate individuals and that they need and want their separate lives and identities. This "normal" individuation phase may be problematic for addicts in recovery when they are taken by surprise by the fact that there are areas of real difference between them and their partner.

The recognition that your partner has their own interests, priorities, tastes, goals, friendships or foibles may be perceived as a threat to the newly formed bond and may trigger your own fear of abandonment. Criticism of each other may become more frequent if you and your partner feel threatened by the emerging independence. This is an effort to get back to a safer place. The recovery mantras that are best suited to this bump in the road are "This too shall pass" and "Easy does it."

Another recovery idea that you are already familiar with is that of *not isolating*. In your addiction you were aware that isolation was not your friend, and in relationships it is very easy for couples to isolate with one another in their relationship, shutting out the outside world. This makes both partners feel both safe and desperate at the same time. Being aware that you will have to have lives outside the relationship is the same awareness and the same recovery skill as reaching out to others in your addiction recovery.

But what if your partner suddenly gets very irritable with something that you have done? What if an attack ensues and you become extremely defensive? It can be very frightening to be confronted with someone else's strong emotions, but in recovery you will have already been learning not to sit in judgment and to give someone space to have whatever feelings they have. You don't have to just accept a torrent of verbal abuse, but you can speak to your partner's feelings rather than launching a counterattack. You can say "I get that such and such drives you nuts," or "I'm sorry" without getting into playing a condescending or phony therapist role. This is the skill of listening. Sometimes in recovery you will hear people talk about "listening" vs. "waiting to talk." Actively listening means paying close attention to what is going on with someone else. This brings into play the recovery skills of focusing on one thing at a time, and of letting go of your ego. My mentor, Michael Alvarez, put it poetically: *"Really listening is like dying for a minute."*

8. The "Attraction to Others" Challenge

This is what you have probably been dreading since the beginning. The moment when you suspect that you or your partner has noticed someone else as attractive or has seemed to show an "interest" in someone. I'm not talking about imaginary fears here; I'm talking about situations in which, in a normal way, one of you finds a third person attractive or appealing in some way.

The first and most important recovery skill in this situation is to remember that *"It's not all about me."* Your partner may think someone else is drop dead gorgeous, but that may have absolutely nothing to do with anything. Another way to put this is "What's it to you??" However, it is a completely different story if you or your partner have engaged in "triangulating," looking at other people or flirting with other people in a way that is guaranteed to be threatening to the partner. It is not always easy to tell when you should be able to detach, and when you should say "Hey, I don't like you doing that!" And it will take some thought and consultation with trusted advisors to regain your balance if you are on the receiving end.

But what if it is *you* that is going around flirting or "intriguing" with others? You may feel that what you are doing is harmless enough, but if it bothers your partner then the bad news is *you can't do it any more*. Now you will be putting into practice in your relationship the idea that you must care for the relationship as you would a young child. The relationship is vulnerable and needs you to put aside your own needs at times. This relates to the recovery idea of the "sacrificial spirit" talked about in the

Twelve Steps and Twelve Traditions of Alcoholics
Anonymous (1952).

9. The Sexual Challenge

Caring for your sexual life in a relationship can be
especially daunting for recovering sex addicts. The old
relationship style for many sex addicts was one of out of
control sexual behavior *outside their relationship* and
difficulty of some sort with sex *in their relationship*. Even
if the relationships in the past began with a heightened
sexual charge, the addict would sooner or later revert to
their "acting out" behavior and become less engaged in sex
with their partner. This is because, as stated above, the sex
addict has struggled with a fundamental inability to put sex
and intimacy together in the same relationship.

Some addicts want to think that they were having normal
sex lives in the past, even though a truly healthy sexual life
was not possible without addressing the addiction. It will
be important to keep a sharp eye on what you are doing and
feeling with regard to sex in your new relationship.

Sometimes the relationship of the addict is with "sex
buddies," where there really is no relationship outside of
the sexual one, or where the sex is the main thing, and any
other kind of activity or commitment is largely absent.
This is reminiscent of the drug addict's "drug buddies" or
the alcoholic's "drinking buddies." What matters in these
relationships is the drug (sex) and not the partner, spouse
or friend.

As a recovering sex addict you will be doing something
new; you will be putting love and commitment together

with sex in one, stable, lasting and almost certainly sexually *exclusive* relationship. I say "exclusive" relationship not out of prudery but because for most if not all recovering sex addicts, their rules for their own sexual sobriety contain words such as "no sex outside of a committed relationship" and/or "no sex with someone I do not think I could ever commit to." This is not because they think casual sex is "wrong" but because it is something that just won't work for *them*, usually because it is too much of a slippery slope.

One of the most common problems that may plague recovering sex addicts in relating to a partner sexually is loss of interest. This can take the form of "boredom," i.e. feeling that sex is not exciting enough, or it can take the form of outright avoidance, a feeling of *aversion to sex with a partner*. Most often the feeling of aversion within a relationship is not due to a lack of sexual attraction to the partner. It is due to the feeling that there is something problematic about it in one way or another.

The problem of aversion to sex with a partner is not limited to partnerships or marriages that existed prior to the addict's getting in recovery. It can easily crop up in new love relationships as well. What is often happening is that the recovering addict in the beginning of a new relationship is still in a kind of *fantasy bubble*. This is unavoidable to some degree, since even if you get to know the person pretty well, you are still having *sex* for the first time and still in a somewhat altered biochemical state. You don't know the person very well sexually yet, and that leaves a lot of room for you to feel something that is a cousin to your old addictive hyperarousal. When this stage is over, you may find that you feel something is missing or different, and that may be experienced as alarming.

Another kind of sexual avoidance experienced by recovering addicts derives from childhood trauma of some sort. One of my sex addict clients who was averse to sex in her marriage described the prospect of sex with her husband as "icky." When asked what that meant, she said that it *felt like incest*, like having sex with a relative, since she had been so close to him for so long. Her way of separating out sex and intimacy was based on the feeling that sex with someone you know is a form of violation.

Many of the techniques and tools commonly used in working with couples who have sexual problems are also applicable to the recovering sex addict. Many of these tools and ideas are discussed at length in the final six chapters of Patrick Carnes' book *Sexual Anorexia* (1997). Recovering sex addicts may be subject to the same hang-ups and cultural influences that impair sexual relationships for non-addicts. The use of specific techniques for being more in touch with yourself and your partner, techniques built around examining anger and gender prejudice, honest communication about or during sex, non-sexual touching, non-genital sex and so on, may help the recovering addict in the same way that they help others.

But recovering sex addicts may have an additional layer of problems relating not only to very deeply-rooted fears but to patterns of sexual arousal and sexual relating that may have been established and reinforced through many years or even decades of practice. I have already discussed some of these particular problems in adjusting to a new paradigm of sexual relating above in Chapter VII, Section 7. In that chapter I touched on the fact that just for openers, sex addicts entering into relationships in recovery may have a big adjustment to make in two areas:

1. They may be unprepared for the fact that their sex life with their partner will not have the same kind of super-charged arousal as their addictive sexual behavior, and

2. They may not fully grasp that the new paradigm involves letting go of orgasm as the main or only point to having sex.

This is not to say that recovering sex addicts and their partners should have low expectations about sex. They may find, as many recovering couples do, that there is enormous passion and joy in sex with their partner. But it is not the same as acting out! What you will come to realize over time is that although the hyperarousal of addictive sexual behaviors is still there in your memory and your imagination, it is becoming more remote. The sex life that you have with a partner will come to feel preferable, if different, from what came before. You are not the same person you were before you became sexually sober, so your sex life won't be the same either.

But what about the challenge of feeling avoidant toward sex in your relationship? I think that a helpful and possibly counterintuitive concept applies to a greater or lesser extent for most recovering sex addicts in their new relationship. It is the recovery tool referred to above as "planning." In the movies we are accustomed to seeing romantic passion portrayed as two people who just met ripping each others clothes off in frenzy. This looks like fun, and it certainly qualifies as "spontaneous." But for recovering sex addicts in relationships *there will be no way of getting used to the new paradigm of sex unless you actually continue to have sex,* after the initial rush has worn off. This is the recovery skill of simply being willing to <u>practice new behavior</u> even when it feels strange or different or a little frightening.

What I am proposing is that if both partners recognize that they enjoy sex together and also recognize that they too often tend to let it go by the way, then they need to *plan to have sex.* This is not to say that you should not also make time for other sensual experiences. But it means *building sex into your plan for your week*, not rigidly of course, but planning when you will have sex and making sure you have the time and space to devote to the experience. This may involve some discussion and negotiation. I can hear some people saying that I am making it sound like an onerous chore. But it is not. It is recognizing that your relationship has a sensual and sexual dimension and that you as a recovering sex addict may be at risk for allowing that aspect of your relationship to become shortchanged.

10. The Marriage Challenge

Marriage presents relationship challenges, and it can also be a "sobriety challenge," especially if you have not done some of the careful work involved in confronting your old patterns, changing your relationship style and improving your relationship skills. But even if your sex addiction sobriety is solid and there is little danger of a relapse on that front, marriage represents more of a giant step than most people realize. It adds a new dimension to your efforts to have and sustain a committed relationship.

In your addiction you may have taken the step of marriage lightly because you convinced yourself that it didn't matter all that much. Partly this may have been due to not really understanding what a good marriage looked like. Even in the larger culture there is confusion about the role of marriage. I have heard supposedly "normal" people say that it didn't matter how attracted they were to their spouse sexually because "Nobody is faithful to their partner in the long run anyway."

Or, as a sex addict you may have married without much of yourself "invested" in the relationship. After all, you had a whole other life that you consciously or unconsciously had no intention of giving up. Since you had less invested in the relationship you had less to lose. This also served to defend against the deep abandonment fear addicts may suffer. Fortunately in recovery you have given up the idea of leading a sexual double life. And as you approached dating and relationships, including renewing an existing relationship, you have hopefully gained a new perspective on commitments: You now see the relationship as having a great deal to offer you. *But there is now a great deal at stake.* As Patrick Carnes has said, "Suddenly everything matters."

Regardless of whether you think it should be, marriage is culturally a big deal. Historically it is a sacrament; Catholics believe it is a relationship that is exempt from original sin. But even if you don't believe in these religious traditions, marriage is a legally binding contract with many implications, as everyone who has drafted a prenuptial agreement can tell you.

You will likely feel that many of the issues you confront as you contemplate your future (or renewed) marriage are some kind of a *test* of something. For example, a couple I know recently decided to get married even though it meant that the wife would give up a significant amount of alimony from her ex-husband. That in turn brought up other questions as to how the couple would handle all kinds of financial issues after they were married.

The good news is that most if not all of the issues that arise when people contemplate marriage are really just practical problems. They need to be viewed as such and they can then be solved. On a practical level you may have to compromise, give up something, and get expert advice.

Most of the *conflicts* that arise prior to an anticipated marriage are due to one or both people allowing themselves to see a practical issue, whatever it is, as a proof of love or as a failure to prove love. When you are planning to get married in recovery you are probably very invested in getting it right, in things "working out." Therefore you are in a somewhat brittle state when things that should be no big deal or easily solved loom large and bring out your worst fears. The couple with the alimony problem above could see the problem as just a thing to work out in some fair way, and ultimately they did but the most immediate reaction for most people in this delicate premarital state is to see things in terms of "If you really loved me you'd...."

As a person in recovery, your best strategy in this seemingly risky situation is to realize that you have the capacity to have faith. Because you have done the work, you have faith in yourself that you can keep your balance and solve problems in an emotionally mature way (or relatively so). You also have faith that the love you share with your partner can be real and lasting. You may have a life history in which love has never been reliable, but now you are operating on a new paradigm; you have decided to trust someone else and trust yourself. You also recognize that things may be difficult, things may change, or that the relationship may not work out, but you now have faith that you will in the long run get what is best for you and that it is OK to take an action without knowing or being able to control the ultimate outcome.

X. The Importance of Core Mindfulness Skills

Wisdom is not a product of thought. The deep knowing that is wisdom arises through the simple act of giving someone or something your full attention. Attention is primordial intelligence, consciousness itself.

Eckhart Tolle, *Stillness Speaks*

Dr. Patrick Carnes has talked about sex addiction as, among other things, an *"Attention Deficit Disorder."* Many abilities such as the ability to be "present in the moment" and to reflect on your own feelings and behaviors, the ability to actively listen to someone else, the ability to be comfortable in your own skin, in fact all the abilities that are involved in relationships in recovery seem to be built on the foundation of being able to *focus your attention.*

Problems that resemble what we think of as Attention Deficit Disorder are also evident in those cases where the person has a traumatic history leading to *dissociative splitting,* or *dissociative avoidance.* In this case the person cannot stay present and focused due to automatic reactions of fear learned earlier in life. They "zone out" or freeze.

As we discussed in Chapter V, most sex addicts have experienced trauma in the form of disturbances in their early attachment bonds to their parents or caretakers. (Sex addiction has also been described as an "attachment disorder.") Secure attachments are believed to be necessary for the development of the integration of cognitive and emotional processes.

Dr. James Masterson (1985), a pioneer in the treatment of personality disorders, saw early trauma and attachment issues as leading to what he called disorders of the "self." He described the disruption of the normal developmental process of separation-individuation of the "self" as it interrelated with the psychoanalytic ego-object relations theory with the ego as the "executive arm" of the self. The failure to develop an individuated self made for (among other things) a *deficit* in what Masterson called the "self-monitoring functions of the ego." He described the self-monitoring functions as:

- Ability to observe your own behavior critically

- Ability to anticipate the results of your actions

- Ability to soothe yourself

- Ability to correct yourself

According to Masterson, the lack of what is sometimes referred to as an "observing ego" results in predictable consequences in the person's life, including potentially:

- Low functioning, marginal functioning

- Self-defeating behaviors

- Self-destructive behaviors

- *Substance abuse and other addictions*

Masterson's school of thought had some success in treating borderline personality disorder by going more or less directly to the traumatic experiences and working them through in psychoanalytic psychotherapy.

Dr. Marsha M. Linehan, a cognitive behavioral psychologist, shares the view that self-destructive and addictive behavior disorders originate in early life trauma and attachment issues but developed her own technique called Dialectical Behavior Therapy (1993). Linehan saw _core mindfulness skills_ as a primary building block for other recovery skills such as emotion regulation, distress tolerance, and interpersonal effectiveness. Possessing these skills, the patient could begin to unravel their underlying childhood trauma and attachment issues.

Most treatment programs for sex addiction today include a combination of techniques to develop self-observation, learn emotion regulation, and provide supports for behavioral accountability.

But you, as a recovering sex addict, may be delving into the world of relationships without having developed core mindfulness skills and/or without having worked through childhood trauma issues. You may be ready to try relationships even though your work in these areas is not fully complete.

I have a client who had history of severe drug and alcohol abuse and severe sexual acting out. Sober from drugs and alcohol for many years, he went through a program of intensive outpatient therapy for sex addiction. Currently he is doing well with his sexual sobriety and using all of the tools available to support his recent sex addiction recovery. He and his wife have gone to a counselor together and have agreed to put their relationship on hold for six months and to work on their own problems separately.

What this client knows is that he is just beginning to be able to feel "*present*," i.e. *mindful* of what he is doing at a given time and able to devote his *attention* to it. He reports that he spends time with his young daughter and that he is now able to attend to her, to focus on her and on what she is feeling in a new way. He is therefore able to be understanding and supportive toward her in a way that he never was before and in a way that his parents never were with him. This in turn has made him connect with the sadness and grief of his own unhappy and stressful childhood which helps him to heal and grow.

Can you begin to date and possibly begin a new relationship even if you have not completely mastered mindfulness and the related skills that support your new relationship style? The answer is "yes." But you will need to continue to practice and improve your abilities in this area to effectively deal with whatever situations arise in your relationship life.

So what are core mindfulness skills, and how can you promote them? According to Dr. Linehan, mindfulness skills involve

- Observing (events and emotions without trying to escape),

- Describing (events and responses in words without projecting),

- Participating (entering completely into the activity of the current moment),

- Taking a nonjudgmental stance (judging something as neither good nor bad),

- Focusing on one thing in the moment (full attention, not splitting attention), and

- Being effective (focus on goals, not on being right).

Not surprisingly, these abilities correlate directly with what you as an addict in recovery may have been exposed to in the course of your treatment, your therapy or your 12-step work. <u>All of these aspects of mindfulness involve the use of *attention*</u> and, to a greater or lesser degree, the ability to let go of "*self will*" (ego) as well as its cousins "*judgments*" *and* "*expectations.*"

In order to "observe" events and emotions, describe them correctly, and participate completely in the activity of the moment you will be using your recovery skills of surrender, acceptance, and self-honesty. If you have delved into some kind of spiritual practice such as meditation or yoga, or if you read books that teach about meditation and mindfulness then you will have that advantage in your attempt to stay centered, appropriately responsive and responsible.

Mindfulness and meditation practice are often talked about in the same breath. "*Mind*" *in this context has a meaning that is different from* "*intellect*" *or* "*verbal thought.*" Dr. Linehan describes the mind of mindfulness as our "Wise Mind." This is a concept akin to "intuition," i.e. a kind of "knowing" that is not the same as reason and that has the quality of what Malcolm Gladwell in his book *Blink* (2005) describes as "rapid cognition," the grasping of meaning without relying on intellectual analysis. Dr. Linehan described "Wise Mind" as neither "reasonable mind" nor "emotion mind" but as a combination of both. This direct, instantaneous knowing has been described as the source of all scientific and artistic inspiration.

Linehan's Wise Mind

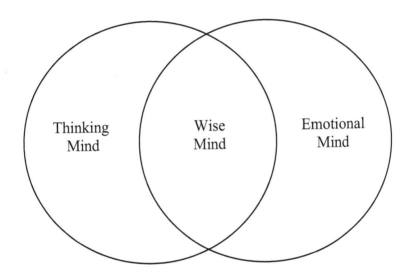

Thinking
Mind

Wise
Mind

Emotional
Mind

In the next chapter we will look at some of the skills and behaviors that characterize healthy intimate relationships, and you will probably notice that they rest not only on all of the recovery skills and relationship skills we have been considering so far, but that they rely ultimately on a new and healthier way of paying attention.

XI. What Do Healthy Relationships Look Like?

...Our love is joyous! Song and laughter are
the flowers of our enduring love!

Giacomo Puccini, *La Boheme*

General Formulations

There has already been a great deal written about what constitutes a healthy intimate relationship. I will only touch on a few of the formulations that have been most often talked about in the context of addiction treatment as they have a lot in common; I will also attempt to highlight the salient points as they apply to relationship recovery for recovering sex addicts and their partners. There are three theorists whose formulas I will describe in outline: John M. Gottman PhD, Terrence T. Gorski M.A. and Patrick J. Carnes PhD. Dr. Gottman's formula is put forth in his book *Seven Principles for Making Marriage Work* (1999); Terrence Gorski's formula is from his book *Addictive Relationships, Why Love Goes Wrong in Recovery* (1993); and Dr. Carnes' formula is from his book *Sexual Anorexia, Overcoming Sexual Self-Hatred* (1997). I will also include the checklist from David H. Olson *et al.* (2007), called FACES III Couples Version, which is used to rate relationships.

Dr. John M. Gottman, a noted therapist, researcher and writer on relationships and marriage has outlined seven key characteristics of happy, emotionally intelligent couples from research he has done over the years. His findings relate to people in general and not only to a particular group such as addicts. His prescriptions are:

1. **Enhance Your Love Map.** This is explained as knowing each other's goals, worries and hopes and as knowing the major events in each other's history and current life.

2. **Nurture Fondness and Admiration.** This has to do with believing your partner is worthy of honor and respect and expressing your fondness and admiration.

3. **Turn Toward Each Other**. This involves giving attention, affection, humor and support.

4. **Let Your Partner Influence You.** Gottman states: "The happiest, most stable marriages are those in which the husband treats his wife with respect and does not resist sharing power and decision making with her."

5. **Solve Your Solvable Problems.** This is described as a 4-step process which includes:

   • Making "I" statements, being polite and not judgmental, and stating your feelings without blame;

   • De-escalating tension, taking a break, sharing your feelings, apologizing, and expressing appreciation;

   • Soothing yourself and each other, and

   • Compromise, i.e. finding the areas of common ground.

6. **Overcome Gridlock.** Unearthing each person's expressed or unexpressed dreams and honoring each others goals and dreams as part of your life together.

7. **Create Shared Meaning.** Creating a micro-culture as a couple with your own customs, ritual, myths and dreams.

Terrence T. Gorski is a researcher in the area of the treatment of addictive and co-addictive disease. His book on relationships in recovery refers to addicts, alcoholics, and other people in recovery but not specifically to sex addiction. He is careful to preface his ideas about healthy relationships with the idea that you cannot have a healthy relationship without working on yourself first. Regarding relationships he describes the following four "Healthy Principles:"

Healthy people know how to get out of relationships responsibly. He emphasizes this because he believes that "When you have no choice, you will never be free to love because love is a free expression of choice." This reminds me of the humorous saying that addicts don't have relationships, they take hostages.

1. Healthy people do not lose themselves in their relationships. We have discussed this issue above in Chapter VI in section 3 which dealt with what you should realistically expect a relationship to do for you and the need to have a separate identity from your partner.

2. Healthy people recognize there are three categories of problems: (a) my problems which I solve on my

own (maybe with support and understanding from my partner), (b) your problems which you solve on your own (ditto support and understanding) and (c) our problems which we must work on together. Gorski believes that in any relationship there are all three present.

3. Healthy people recognize that there is no such thing as a perfect relationship. This has to do with taking a long view and seeing the process as one of progressive developmental growth.

In addition to the "healthy principles," Gorski puts forth Ten Steps to Healthy Intimacy. They are:

1. Establish and maintain a program of personal growth and recovery (and don't have relationships until you get your stuff together.)

2. Establish realistic expectations of what an intimate relationship is and should be.

3. Select an appropriate partner.

4. Spend time with your partner, meaning alone with each other *and* socially as a couple.

5. Share life experiences—the more the better.

6. Share the breadth of your experiences, i.e. talk about what you did without the other person.

7. Learn how to balance risk-taking and comfort-seeking.

8. Learn to talk about two things: what you believe you need and what you want in a relationship.

9. Learn to problem-solve together.

10. Make your partner psychologically visible. By this he means telling your partner what he or she means to you and how you feel about him/her.

Dr. Patrick Carnes (1997) describes seven "intimacy dimensions." For each of these he gives six or eight examples. I will paraphrase some of these to give you the idea of what each dimension stands for.

- Initiative (reaching out, expressing feelings and taking risks)

- Presence (listening, paying attention to others, being available)

- Closure (resolving things, acknowledging others, expressing thanks)

- Vulnerability (sharing problems, sharing your process, getting input)

- Nurturance (empathy, caring statements, support, empowering others)

- Honesty (not hiding deep feelings, being clear about disagreements)

- Play (joy, laughter, adventurousness, valuing leisure time, smelling the roses)

Olsen *et. al.* (2007) put forth the following 20 items from the *Family Adaptability and Cohesion Evaluation Scale III*:

1. We ask each other for help.
2. When problems arise, we compromise.
3. We approve of each other's friends.
4. We are flexible in how we handle our differences.
5. We like to do things with each other.
6. Different persons act as leaders in our marriage.
7. We feel closer to each other than to people outside our family.
8. We change our way of handling tasks.
9. We like to spend free time with each other.
10. We try new ways of dealing with problems.
11. We feel very close to each other.
12. We jointly make the decisions in our marriage.
13. We share hobbies and interests together.
14. Rules change in our marriage.
15. We can easily think of things to do together as a couple.
16. We shift household responsibilities from person to person.
17. We consult each other on our decisions.
18. It is hard to identify who the leader is in our marriage.
19. Togetherness is a top priority.
20. It is hard to tell who does which household chores.

Healthy Relating as a Result, Not a Cause

So what are we to make of these descriptions? Are these things we can practice and get better at? Probably. Are they things we should keep in mind? Definitely. How else should we use these reflections on healthy relating?

However, my own feeling is that as accurate as the above formulas are they are not things that can be taught in the usual way. I see them as a result of a learning process, a manifestation of a good relationship rather than as a program for creating one.

If we do the initial self-exploration, if we do our thinking and planning, if we are conscientious in our observing and taking stock as we go along, and if we learn to stay aware enough to gradually feel more safe and loving, then the transformation from addictive to healthy relationships will take place over time as a relationship develops. If we are able to utilize our spiritual skills as described in Chapter XIII we will be in a position to maintain these positive ways of being in a relationship because we will have established a default position of connection with ourselves and our partner and a standard of loving kindness.

If you go back to Chapter IV and look at your relationship timeline, you will realize that even before you had the tools of recovery, part of you was attempting to change in a positive direction. All the more do I have confidence in you, the person in recovery, that you have already developed a repertoire of skills and tools, which you have learned to use, that you rely on trusted advisors, and that you have developed a life habit of self-exploration and an urge toward healthier connecting with people.

I have confidence that you have only to follow through with the planning and using of the tools and maintain the spiritual skills discussed in Chapter XIII in order to develop in the area of relationships. Once you are aware that relationships need care and feeding, and once you begin to apply your existing recovery skills as you have done in the preceding chapters, you can rely on that momentum to keep you working in a positive direction, a direction of strength and health.

What is a "Good" Relationship?

I have heard it said that a "good" relationship is one you learn from. Inherent in this idea is the fact that most people have more than one close relationship in their lives. *If each new relationship (or even each renewal of an old relationship) is no different from what went before then you have not learned and grown.* As we will discuss further in Chapter XIII, there is a great deal to be learned from a "failed" relationship and **when we do this learning, the failed relationship is more successful than a stable but spiritually stagnant one.**

Also inherent in this idea of relationships as a learning process is the notion that relationships are good or bad *not* in terms of how long you can stay together or how well you function as a couple in public, but rather should be looked at as *a process of your and your partner's emotional growth or lack of it.* In this situation the inner growth is in the strengths and abilities which allow you to continue to experience a loving, nurturing and contented connection with a partner.

Your Relationship Evolution

You might try now looking at your old Relationship Inventory from Chapter IV and listing for each relationship the things you were able to learn about yourself, your way of relating, and what you needed to change. You will be able to tell this as you look down the list of relationships because it will become apparent to you that you in the next relationship you were attempting, whether successfully or not, to change the scenario in some way. True, you may have unconsciously played out the same old script, but if you noticed even that you had some intention to change, then you can give yourself credit for having grown from that relationship in some degree.

A good example is the way some people try to pick a different kind of partner and end up finding out they are exactly the same as the old choices in basic ways. Another example is that some people do opt for a different kind of relationship, say one that is less sexually addictive, only to find that they then begin to engage in other addictions such as overeating. But the point is that at least they had a *partial awareness that something needed to change* and they were trying to apply something they had learned.

List your relationships (who with, what time period) then underneath write anything you learned even if it seems silly. Then under that write how that learning may have influenced your next relationship choice and/or behavior.

1. Relationship:_____

    What Learned:_____

_____

Attempted to Change Next Time:_____

_____

2. Relationship:_____

What Learned:_____

_____

Attempted to Change Next Time:_____

_____

3. Relationship:_____

What Learned:_____

_____

Attempted to Change Next Time:_____

_____

4. Relationship:_____

What Learned:_____

_____

Attempted to Change Next Time:_____

_____

5. Relationship:_____

What Learned:_____

_____

Attempted to Change Next Time:_____

_____

XII. Relationship Relapse or Slip Scenarios

Now is the time for one of you to be gracious,
To allow a kindness beyond thought and hurt.

John O'Donohue, *To Bless the Space Between Us*

Let's suppose that you have completed most of the tasks in the earlier chapters: that you have done the work of becoming the kind of person with the kind of awareness that will enable you to have a good relationship. Let's further assume that you have found (or re-discovered) a partner who does not fit your old addictive relationship scenario, that your relationship has survived the common relationship challenges in Chapter IX, and that you and he or she have already confronted some of the basic areas for change in Chapter VI and have grappled with and probably continue to grapple with the basic relationship dilemmas in Chapter VII as your relationship evolves.

At this point you feel like a whole new world has opened up to you and you are beginning to see how wonderful the fruits of recovery really are. What could go wrong? Maybe nothing, but as recovering sex addicts we know that it cannot hurt to look ahead at some of the future situations that could derail your progress.

A Relapse Scenario in sex addiction treatment is an attempt to inoculate yourself against slipping backward by making a calculated prediction as to a sequence of events that could lead you back into an old behavior. In other words it enables you to see it coming and to change course. In this way you will not be taken by surprise and act in automatic or unconscious ways in response to unanticipated "triggers."

We will borrow the Relapse Scenario idea from addiction treatment and modify it for the purpose of identifying possible ways that old behavior patterns can creep in and sabotage the harmony and mutual support you experience in your intimate relationship. We will use the word *"slip"* instead of *"relapse"* to indicate that even when you revert to old behaviors in a relationship, you always have the option to repair and recover the ground you have lost. These slips are not the same as slipping into your old sex addiction behaviors.

This scenario will be very individual to you. You could begin by looking at your "Middle Circle" behaviors in your relationship circle plan, the "slippery" behaviors and situations you wish to avoid. But a true Slip Scenario goes beyond that. It begins with a life event or a stress that has the potential to set in motion a cascade of other situations which can end in a "slip" or "relapse," that is a situation in which you sabotage yourself and do some real damage to your relationship.

Types of Life Stressors

The following are examples of types of life stressors that you might be able to anticipate for the purpose of the Relapse Scenario exercise.

1. Life Crises and Life Changes

For a practicing sex addict the stress might be getting out of bed and finding that you are out of coffee! This is obviously unlikely to cause a relapse for you at this stage of your recovery. But how will you identify the initial stressor? Any life crisis or major life change is a good candidate. Even good things like the birth of a child could potentially set in motion a problematic chain of behavior and conflict. But certainly other life changes and crises that are not uncommon could be things you want to anticipate such as moving, promotions, someone quitting work, going back to work, getting more absorbed in their work, illness, injury, turmoil in your extended family and so on.

2. Lifestyle Imbalance

Another type of precipitating stress that you could consider would be that of an event which throws you out of "lifestyle balance" (for more on lifestyle balance see the "Personal Craziness Index" in Patrick Carnes' *Facing the Shadow* (2010). You have neglected an important area of your life, an activity or support system that you need to stay on an even keel.

3. Multiple Addictions

And another and often major stress to a relationship in recovery would be the emergence or re-emergence of *another addiction* as a problem in one or the other partner. Most sex addicts, indeed most addicts of any kind exhibit one or more other addictions at various times in their lives. For example you may suddenly find that you (or your partner) are spending to excess, getting the family into debt in an out-of-control way.

A Hypothetical Chain of Events

At the point when a crisis or change occurs you might be justified in being irritable or unreasonable to some extent, you might be emotionally exhausted and not be thinking clearly. You might act in a way that is selfish or inconsiderate, even hurtful. Normally if that happened and your relationship had been strong beforehand, you would probably bounce back, repair any damage or hurt feelings and re-establish your equilibrium and your healthy bond. It might take some thought and it might take some talking to your trusted advisors or even a therapist to help you through this rough period in your lives together.

But what if you don't bounce back, and you don't get the needed help and advice? Let's say you are away on business and you don't really want to go back to whatever situation awaits you at home. Let's say you decide to *take an extra day or two* to yourself. Here is a choice point. You could ask your partner if he or she minds if you get away for a day or two, or you could just decide that you are going to do it anyway, regardless of what your partner wants. Let's say for the sake of the scenario that you do the latter. Having practiced many good relationship skills you know that it is of some significance to your partner to have his or her feelings taken into consideration in this kind of situation.

Next you return home with a stained relationship and a family crisis or stressor that is still lingering. *If you are lucky*, your partner will insist on confronting the issue and working it through! But what if that doesn't happen for whatever reason? What is the next step in this hypothetical downward spiral? One possibility is that you enter into a period of being "pleasant" to one another and keeping your interaction confined to *trivial conversation*. You keep the daily life of the household going but you are quite distanced from one another. Nobody is happy or comfortable.

This unresolved and alienated situation may not ever resolve itself, or it may take a long time before you and your partner can function in a healthy way together. In the meantime one or both of you may compensate by doing negative, self-destructive, addictive or passive-aggressive behaviors. You are probably feeling cool or even angry, you are probably not able to be sexual and affectionate, and you are barely talking. You have had a relationship "slip."

Slip Scenario Diagram

On the following pages are two sample relationship Slip Scenarios showing the deteriorating situation by virtue of the statements on the top of each step or "choice point." Underneath each step is listed the alternative behavior that could help avert the downward trend. Make your own Relapse Scenario based on what you already know about yourself and your relationship patterns.

Relationship Slip Scenario Example 1

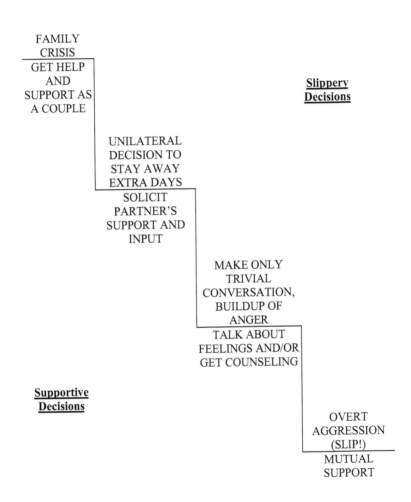

Relationship Slip Scenario Example 2

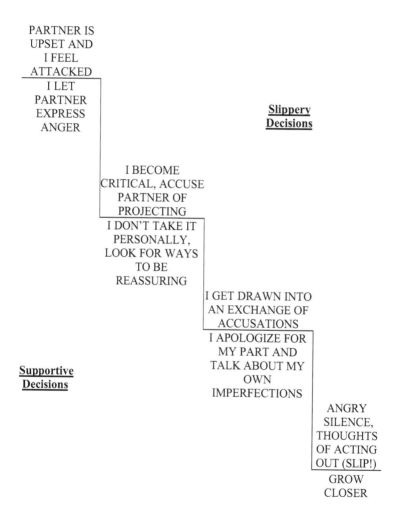

PARTNER IS
UPSET AND
I FEEL
ATTACKED

I LET
PARTNER
EXPRESS
ANGER

**Slippery
Decisions**

I BECOME
CRITICAL, ACCUSE
PARTNER OF
PROJECTING

I DON'T TAKE IT
PERSONALLY,
LOOK FOR WAYS
TO BE
REASSURING

I GET DRAWN INTO
AN EXCHANGE OF
ACCUSATIONS

I APOLOGIZE FOR
MY PART AND
TALK ABOUT MY
OWN
IMPERFECTIONS

**Supportive
Decisions**

ANGRY
SILENCE,
THOUGHTS
OF ACTING
OUT (SLIP!)

GROW
CLOSER

Your Relationship Slip Scenario

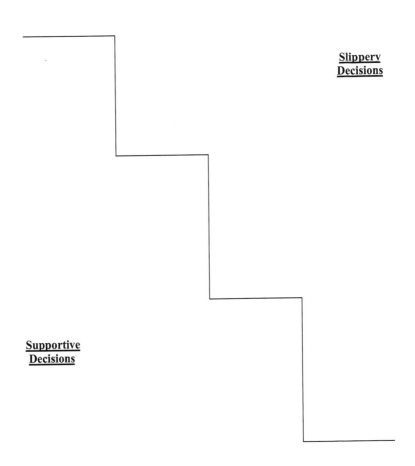

Slippery Decisions

Supportive Decisions

Summary: Slips, Relapse, Betrayal and Loyalty

In your sex addiction, a slip is a sexual behavior that is characteristic of you in your addiction. A slip may arise out of an automatic reaction to a situation based on very early conditioning and without any conscious thought or emotion leading up to it. But in recovery you will have learned what situations trigger those automatic reactions, and will have become very good at avoiding putting yourself in those situations. Additionally, you will have become expert at devising strategies to prevent yourself from having an automatic reaction when you know that a potentially "triggery" situation is coming. These situations are individual to you, but very commonly include things like business travel, your spouse being gone or family holiday gatherings.

In relationships, a slip consists of problematic behaviors that were typical of your style of relating while you were active in your sexual addiction such as hostility, put-downs, avoidance, dishonesty, over-control, and so on. Slippery behavior in relationships is reverting to these old defensive behaviors and is triggered by emotional reactions. As we discussed in Chapter V, emotional reactivity to a partner or stressor in a relationship is based on a pattern laid down in early life. Sudden or unexpected emotional reactions such as fear, paranoia, guilt and helplessness can trigger old habits of defensive relating. Becoming aware of your emotions before they can lead you into defensive behavior is an important relationship recovery skill. Awareness of what is going on in your body is the best way to identify these harmful emotions. The emotions that reflect early reactions to stress or trauma in childhood will likely be experienced by your body before they are translated into words and categorized by your mind.

When you feel a negative emotion overtaking your body, such as a sudden agitation, a sudden feeling of paralysis or a wave of negativity that feels like a tightening inside of you, taking a couple of breaths and using the mindfulness skills described above in Chapter X is crucial to creating a sliver of separation between your unconscious emotional reaction and your conscious mind. It is what allows your mind to then utilize your recovery skills to reflect on the situation and behave in a conscious and constructive way.

What constitutes *betrayal* in a relationship? Leaving aside the question of what your partner might perceive as a betrayal or not, a working definition of a betrayal would be:

"Taking an important part of yourself away from your intimate relationship and giving it to someone or something else with an element of deception."

For example, if you have to have dinner with a colleague to talk business (let's say you are a straight male and your colleague is too) and you tell your partner you cannot invite her, she may not like it, but it is not a betrayal. If she is afraid you two are going to go to a strip club together, and you can honestly say that that is never going to happen, then it is not a betrayal, even if she is still fearful. If you "honestly" don't think that you will go to a strip club, but deep down you sense that that may be a possibility, then it is a form of betrayal. You have lied to yourself.

In another example, if you lie and say that the dinner is with a male colleague when it is with a female colleague, then it is a betrayal. What about if you admit that you are having dinner with a female colleague and tell your partner that it is all business but you don't say that the female colleague happens to be attractive? What if you are just *"not thinking about"* whether the female colleague is attractive to you? This too constitutes a betrayal. Why? Although you are not consciously deceiving your partner, you are *lying to yourself.* You are not looking at what you are doing in an objective manner and are allowing yourself to make excuses: "Nothing is going to happen. What's the difference if I find her attractive, I'll never act on it," etc. This example is a slippery pattern in that it not only threatens the integrity of the relationship, it threatens your sexual sobriety as well. Deceiving yourself or your partner is not good for any relationship, but it has greater potential consequences for relationships in recovery.

What should we call "disloyalty?" Not all disloyalty is betrayal. Disloyalty may be present in any situation in which you disregard the feelings and needs of your partner. It can also be present when you place more importance on some other relationship than on your relationship with your partner. On the other hand, all betrayal can be safely said to be disloyal in that it contains the element of deception.

With regard to sex addiction slips and relapses, i.e., engaging in your old addictive behavior such as Internet pornography, they may or may not be a form of betrayal. If your partner is privy to what is going on inside of you when you feel in danger of a slip into your old acting out behavior, then there is a basis for dealing with slips and even relapses in a healthy way if they do happen. Let's say you tell your partner that you saw someone or something that brought up old addictive fantasies for you. In this situation you are being honest from the start and you are treating your addiction as a problem that needs to be dealt with. The fact that you and your partner can see the experience as part of your "illness" provides reassurance that you can and will deal with it appropriately and conscientiously.

XIII. Relationships as Spiritual Practice

*He was free, but too infinitely free; not striding upon the
earth but floating above it. He felt the lack in him of that
weight of human relations ... those thousand ties that bind
him to others and lend density to his being.*

Antoine de Saint-Exupery, *Wind, Sand and Stars*

Sex addiction is often seen as a spiritual disease

The sense in which sex addiction is a spiritual disease is
probably best understood in terms of it being a state of
disconnection, or *unconsciousness.* In this state we are
acting on ideas and impulses that arise from our
"conditioning," our early formative experiences, rather
than what is actually going on today. In this sense we are
unaware or disconnected from reality, and we view ourselves and other people through this filter of ingrained
ideas, fears, and expectations. In earlier chapters we have
discussed how these "old" ways of thinking and feeling
are formed in early life and how they hinder us from connecting with ourselves and other people.

The process of becoming spiritually alive or awake can be
seen as that of developing a basic trust in ourselves and
our own intuition. Patrick Carnes (1997) said "Emptying
ourselves of distractions, preoccupation, and obsessions

allows us to connect with who we really are...It is finding the sacred within us. When we are true to ourselves, we are most spiritual."

Trusting ourselves lays the groundwork for trusting others and trusting that "the universe will, in its own way, look after you and protect you, like the lilies of the field..." (Forstater, 2001). Recovery is seen as a process of "spiritual awakening" because it brings us back to awareness of present-moment reality and back to an experience of caring and connectedness.

In all programs of recovery from addiction there is a "spiritual" component of connecting – with one's self, with other people and with a "Higher Power" (or however you conceive it: "The Universe," "Being," "Intuition," "Love," or "God.") And the spiritual component is there because it is through this connection that we get in touch with present day reality and become free of our unconscious conditioning built on the old pain from the past.

In addition to incorporating a "spiritual awakening" into the program of addiction recovery, most programs also contain the idea of going on to live our life in a way that will allow us to continue to live in this "awakened" or aware state and not to slip back into acting on our conditioning. To continue to live our life along "spiritual" lines means that we will be able to enjoy life, that we will be able to use our gifts and that we will be a force for good in the world. This means that we will continue to grow and thrive and help others and not just that we will be free of our addiction.

Failed Relationships and Spiritual Failing

Many recovering sex addicts are able to operate in a very spiritual way in certain spheres of their lives *other than their relationships.* They may be able to completely lose themselves in the creative aspects of their work, feeling very connected, focused and in touch with the "vast intelligence" outside themselves. They may be able to connect with some friends, with children, or with animals in a way that demonstrates deep selflessness, intimacy and grace. And still they may have an essentially addictive pattern of relating to a spouse or partner in an intimate relationship.

The fact is the leftover unconscious baggage from childhood has the more directly to do with intimacy and love relationships than anything else in our lives because these are the relationships that most directly bring up material from our damaged love relationships in childhood.

As a therapist I have notice over the years that many people who seek help have pervasive problems in their lives, but by far the most common kind of client in my experience was someone who would not have defined themselves as needing psychological help and would not have shown up in a counselor's office except for the fact that they were having great trouble finding or sustaining a love relationship. Usually they appeared for therapy soon after a relationship ended and they were confronted with all the old pain again. And if they found a new lover fairly soon then they might quit therapy, feeling that now their problems were over.

When you are in your old addictive relationship style, your relating to your partner has a lot in common with all other addictions that are built on old unconscious patterns of dealing with painful emotions. Addictive relationship styles are not spiritually sound because they are attempts to use the relationship in some direct or indirect way to cover over feelings of unhappiness or inadequacy. When the relationship (inevitably) fails to do this, negative feelings return in a way that is analogous to withdrawal from a drug. If the relationship continues anyway, it may take the form of one or another of the dysfunctional relationship styles described in Chapter II. In this case the relationship with a partner is there to support your search for another drug (including sexual) inside or outside the relationship which provides escape from painful feelings.

It is perhaps a difficult point to grasp that on a spiritual level, relationships are not there to make you happy or to save you, but that they are there to allow you to learn to be more conscious.

Relationships provide an opportunity to become increasingly aware and in touch with all the feelings that they bring up. *So confronting a failing relationship and coming to the awareness that basic internal change is needed can be seen as itself a deeply spiritual experience. You might say that failed relationships serve the important function of forcing you (if you are lucky) to confront your own pain, addictiveness and intimacy disability.*

How relationships in recovery are a form of spiritual practice.

Eckhart Tolle in *Practicing the Power of Now* (1999) says:

> How many people does it take to make your life into a spiritual practice? Never mind if your partner will not cooperate…You do not need to wait for the world to become sane, or for somebody else to become conscious, before you can be enlightened. You may wait forever.

What the above quotation means is that you can practice your spiritual skills as you deal with situations that arise in your relationship, and you can do this regardless of whether your partner is engaged in the process or not. In fact as a recovering sex addict you will almost certainly have to use your spiritual skills, and grow in your ability to do so, in order to stay conscious and nurture your love. *So using your relationship as a spiritual practice is about what goes on inside of you and how you behave as a result.*

When people think of a "spiritual practice" they often think of meditation or participation in some religious or spiritual activity or ritual. Taking time for such activities may be an important part of your life in recovery. "Spiritual Practice" may also mean staying connected with a fellowship and with trusted mentors who can help you stay centered. All of the above will be important for you as a recovering addict as you adjust to a new relationship style of contentment and loving kindness. But as elements of the old paradigm try to rear their heads you will need to use your arsenal of spiritual techniques to use to stay centered, aware and level-headed.

The important spiritual skills that come into play in intimate relationships have to do with

- Acceptance,
- Non-reactivity,
- Not judging

Acceptance

This idea will be familiar to you from recovery programs, the idea of accepting things as they are. It is also the same basic idea as the *mindfulness or presence* we discussed in

Chapter X. This means that you practice the skill of "observing" what you are feeling, even if what you are feeling is negative. You watch and you listen, especially to your own emotions. This level of mindfulness applies to a situation in which your partner becomes upset too. Not that you "observe" your partner, although you may do that too, but that you notice and attend to what feelings your partner's reactions are creating *in you* before you do anything else.

Not accepting what is going on inside you takes you away from yourself and renders you powerless to deal with your feelings in a conscious way. *Acceptance has everything to do with stillness and non-action.* The opposite is to *fight* what you feel and in so doing become unconscious and ineffective. If something upsetting happens and you feel irritated, angry or hurt, the first thing to do is to be aware of it, i.e., give it your full attention, and realize that you *are* the awareness; the feeling is just a feeling. As the saying goes, "Be the watcher not the feeling."

This kind of inner awareness is an essential spiritual practice in relationships because it allows you to immediately take your attention off of your partner and put it on yourself. It is this level of mindfulness that allows you to practice the next two spiritual skills in your relating.

Non-Reactivity

The second skill of being non-reactive means that you have already identified a feeling which had the potential to evoke an unconscious reaction and because of this awareness you now have a choice as to what to do or not do about it. Non-reacting means that you will not do what you might have done in the past, i.e., become defensive, attack or make accusations.

Once you know you are upset, then you have the option to make a choice. Spiritually speaking, the first choice you will need to make is to give yourself *the space to calm the feeling,* to self-soothe. As you get better at it, this could be done in as little as a breath or two. Next, and this is important too, you will have to decide in the moment *not* to take a reactive position toward *yourself.* Not to feel guilty or ashamed at yourself for having whatever feelings you have. You will not lash out at your partner in an unconscious way but you will also not lash out at yourself.

I have seen many examples of sex addicts in recovery who when they are emotionally "triggered" by a situation with a partner or lover will pull back (appropriately) but then will continue to withdraw into themselves to "process" this feeling. Even though they don't "react," they *stay upset* and become more upset as they allow themselves to be flooded with disturbing images and feelings from the past. Eventually this process dies down and they can return to the relationship, but they have allowed their reactions to take over and seriously separate them from the present and from their partner, not to mention other ways this may impair their functioning.

In the above example the person has not been able to overcome the early traumatic experiences and their flooding with emotion is definitely real. But *on a spiritual level* they are not dissolving the past because the notion of themselves as a "traumatized victim" has become a principal part of their identity. In such cases it is not through continual reliving of pain that they will become available to intimacy, it is through recognizing *that they are holding onto the pain as a perverse form of self-worth, a part of their ego identity.* In other words they have not done the work of being able to be present, especially to be present to (i.e. aware of) the way in which feeling victimized and in pain are "important" to their sense of self. They become aware that they are in an old familiar state of distress but then they immediately become *unconscious*, and it is downhill from there.

This illustrates that the spiritual skill of "presence" or "mindfulness" continues to be important in every aspect of the other skills. And this has no more *basic* utility in recovery than that of being able to stay present when an emotion emerges and not look for a way to run away from it, either physically or mentally. *To remain stable in the face of unpleasant feelings* is one way to look at the concept of "serenity."

Not Judging

Not judging is an essential spiritual skill that relies on "acceptance" of what <u>is</u> without putting judgments on it. This in turn involves letting go of the ego's need to continually label and judge everything. Labeling and judging is how our minds are programmed to work. They seem to be like popcorn machines, continually throwing out a barrage of labels to place on things. This process then crowds out the possibility of experiencing the world around us and the people around us in a more direct, unfiltered way.

When I used to do mindfulness skills training with a group of adolescents, we used an exercise where we put several small objects in separate paper bags. The objects were common items but it was impossible to tell exactly what they were without looking at them. We passed the bags around the group and asked the members to feel each one and experience how it felt without being able to know what it was. This proved almost impossible. The group members all tended to shout out the names of things that they thought the objects might be, rather than being able to relax and explore the sensations without verbal labels. This exercise shows dramatically how our minds want to gain control of things by identifying them with names. And of course the next step once we identify the thing (or event or experience) is to want to judge it as good or bad, relevant or irrelevant, important, dangerous, etc. etc.

Labels are what allow us to judge, and in relationships they allow us to judge our partner or ourselves. Judgments are what allow us to become angry, frightened and defensive. Judgments take our attention off of our own inner experience and put it on something else. Judgments disconnect us from someone we love and prevent them from changing and growing in the process.

What if your partner acts unconsciously, selfishly or in a way that makes you feel hurt or betrayed? Suppose your partner gets upset and attacks you verbally, accuses you of things or puts you down? No doubt you will be upset by this. You may feel angry, scared, or any number of things. At that point you have an opportunity to practice your spiritual skills in your relationship. You can practice keeping your attention on your own feelings but not allowing them to cause you to reflexively counter-attack. But what then?

You can look at your partner's behavior and instead of labeling it and judging them, you can simply take in what they are doing and feeling. In order to do this you will need to use your other skill of being "present" and "mindful" in relation to this other person. This does not mean being phony "calm" or standing around analyzing them. It just means allowing them to express whatever it is without letting yourself judge them for it. You may not agree with what they are saying, and you may not enjoy being berated, but you can practice letting go of the need to "do" something about it. It is what it is.

On the other hand *you* may have something to express that you are afraid your partner will disagree with or have strong feelings about. Here you will need to practice being non-judgmental about yourself. If you have a feeling or a thought then you are allowed to say it. It is just a feeling. As long as you are not busy arguing with yourself about whether it is "justified" or "picky" or other labels you might place on it, it has no power to create turmoil. If you do not judge yourself in this situation then you do not expect a "satisfactory" answer or a certain result. Applying labels and judgments to yourself and others are two sides of the same coin. Letting go of the need to judge yourself and your partner is a profound and effective practice. When you accept someone as they are, they begin to change.

Meditations for Relationships

Love is a state of being

If I love you then I love you even when you are doing something that feels hurtful. I don't have to like everything you do to have love in me, I only need to know that I can look at the situation with detachment and feel that I know how to stick up for myself if I need to. I also know that telling you that I felt hurt or betrayed is something I should do when I can do it without blaming you. If I feel love in me I will be able to listen to you when you are doing things I don't like. Think of the saying "If you knew all you would pardon all."

Worrying about bumps in the road

It is easy to get spun out worrying about what might not be working right, especially in a new relationship. These are moments when "easy does it" is really important to remember. A new relationship can bring up my craziest moments, moments of exaggerated fear that things are going horribly wrong. In my black-and white addict thinking, I feel that every minor hitch is going to be a deal breaker and sometimes the feeling is overwhelming. I need to let go of the impulse to make everything go smoothly and decide to just wait and see what happens. I need to tell myself, and you, "We'll get through this."

People are different

How am I dwelling on the things I think my partner has to change? Even if my partner wants to change or needs to change in some way, I have to remember the saying "Is this really any of my business?" I may sound corny but the most helpful thing I can do is to accept that my partner *is* another person with their own Higher Power and their own journey. I have to make peace with the fact that if I want to enjoy a great relationship it will be with someone who has many characteristics that are quite different from me. I need to stay interested in and curious about those differences without trying to analyze them or change them.

Expressing loving kindness

What is loving kindness? The Buddha said "Gifts are great, the founding of temples is meritorious, meditations and religious exercises pacify the heart, comprehension of the truth leads to Nirvana – but greater than all is loving-kindness." What can I do today to express loving kindness toward my love? This will bring a surprising kind of serenity to my day. What I need to do is something that will be freely given and that will bring joy or reduce stress. It may be a small thing or a big thing but it will show that I know my partner and pay attention to who they are.

Something is wrong

If I feel a lack in my life it is easy to see it as somehow my partner's fault. If he or she does not provide the kind of companionship I would like in some area of my life, if we prefer different activities, read different kinds of books, I can feel lonely or unfulfilled, especially if there is no immediate way for me to fill that void. To be content today I will have to remind myself to let go of expectations. If I can make some space then something will arrive to fill it. Melody Beattie said, "Embrace the void." If I am preoccupied with what I'm not getting I will be unable to enjoy the day and closed to new experiences. It's my life; there is no way I'm going to get left out of it.

Fighting battles in my head

The argument in the head is something that can be as draining as it is hard to escape. It often comes when I feel somehow powerless in a situation that is causing some kind of trouble or that I'm afraid will cause trouble in the future. Very often the thing I'm am worried about will never come to pass. So first I need to let go of the outcome and focus on accepting the reality of what is. The saying "Accept it, change it or leave it" may be most appropriate here. If I cannot accept the thing, whatever it is, then I need to be able either to change it or leave it. Imaginary battles in my head won't accomplish anything. I need to find some stillness inside myself first and foremost. Quiet my mind, then look to see if I am really powerless or not.

Love is attention

When I give my full unfiltered attention to someone or something, I am expressing love. This is especially true in intimate relationships. When I pay attention to my partner

I am using all of my spiritual capabilities of stillness, acceptance, and most of all, letting go of my own ego. I am also using my relationship skills of listening and awareness. Children know when they are getting our full attention, dogs definitely know it, and some people even believe that plants know it. But it works in reverse also. When post-surgery patients have a plant in their hospital room they recover faster. When they care for the plant they recover even faster still. Attending to someone brings grace to both of us. Some time during the day it is important for me to give my partner my full attention.

What is my duty?

All relationships come with duties, even intimate relationships. The idea that we will always give freely of ourselves to a relationship and never do anything out of a sense of duty is unrealistic. If I do something out of duty does it mean I will inevitably feel resentful later? No, because it depends how I do the thing. I can do something because I believe it is my duty even if it goes against my personal wishes at the moment. I would certainly skip the gym class and go to the hospital if my partner were in an accident. And I would not resent doing it because I would be clear about the fact that I needed to do it. The hard part is figuring out what and when something is my duty. But fortunately I get to decide this. Deciding what things are my duties is a valuable daily practice because when I do this then it is me deciding freely, it is my choice. If I am choosing to do it there is nothing to resent.

Jealousy

Nobody wants to admit that they are feeling jealous. It is as if I am admitting to a defect of character. If I make my partner jealous I will think it is a bad thing. I will want to examine my own behavior and motives very carefully and be willing to listen to what my partner needs me to do. If I feel jealous myself and I trust my partner, I can say something about it. For example, I can say that I feel threatened by something my partner is doing. I can say that I would like them not to do it. That is all I can do. Basically it will be up to them to sort out what they are doing. Jealousy is not a good feeling and I have a right to feel hurt when someone else's unconscious behavior brings it up. But does their behavior really mean anything? Before I get spun out on my own fears I need to use the slogan "what do I *really know?*" I need to use my skill of detachment from someone else's problem, of letting go.

Wishing good things for my partner

This is a powerful spiritual practice whether things in my relationship are going badly or well. Wishing good things for my partner does not only mean wishing for them to be fulfilled, happy or safe. It means wishing for them to have the things they want, regardless of whether they are things I think they should want. Very often the art of compromise in a relationship depends on blind good will: the ability to accept that my partner's wishes are valid even when I cannot at all understand why something is important to them. This involves not only good will and the willingness to compromise but an implicit awareness that my partner is another person, a person different from me in many ways. Wishing good things for my partner helps me to accept and appreciate these differences.

Letting go of outcomes

Of the things that are going on now in my life, what things can I let go of today? There are many potential outcomes in a day and many things I may be apprehensive about. It is always a good practice to consciously let go any of those outcomes that are out of my hands. Most of what other people are going to do is something that is out of my hands. Trying to influence such outcomes is what Al-Anon calls "forcing solutions." If I know I am prone to this I will increase my overall serenity level by a great deal if I practice relinquishing control. One outcome that I may try to grasp at is the outcome of the relationship itself. There are many influences over the outcome of the relationship that are out of my control. Will my partner leave me? It could happen. If I can let go of that outcome I will be practicing leading a surrendered life and as a result, things will undoubtedly go better.

Learning from my partner

Allowing myself to learn from my partner can be threatening. I may feel that if my partner has something to teach me then it must be that I am deficient in something. If my partner knows more than I do then I may feel that I am less desirable, and that in turn may bring up abandonment fear. Logically I know that of course my partner knows more about some things than I do. I need to notice when this threatens me and practice staying open and taking in what he/she has to say.   If I do this I will profit four ways: I will almost certainly learn something; I will overcome my fear of being vulnerable; I will be allowing us to be closer; and, as an extra bonus I will be practicing my skill of really listening.

Stillness together

Writers sometimes talk about two people "lapsing into a companionable silence."   When I think of this it is clear that the periods of comfortable silence between me and another person are a very good barometer of the fact that we are able to be close in a special way.   It is only with someone I have a particular bond with that I don't feel the need to keep up a conversation.   Talking can be a way to connect, but talking is not compatible with stillness.   Having some stillness in my day is essential to my personal growth and spiritual well-being.   When I am still by myself I am rejuvenated.   When I am still with someone else I sometimes feel we are both connecting with something larger than ourselves.   I need to find stillness in order to find serenity.

What is a Oneness?

There is a you, a me and an us.   The us is something in its own right, something that has grown up over time.   In part it is our history together, things we have been through and common concerns.   It is also the level of honesty that we have achieved that allows us to be at ease with each other in a special way.   It is also knowing each other very well and being comfortable in making room for our similarities and our differences. And it is our shared "mythology" of how we met and the particular narrative of our life together. I think most of all it is experiencing the same meanings in things together. I have heard it said that "love is not gazing into each other's eyes; it is gazing together at something else."

Self-awareness

We talk a lot about the ability to be aware of our feelings and to allow ourselves to experience them and express them in a modulated way. Yet, our spirituality is telling us that we must let go of our "self" in the sense of our ego, that our feelings are just there; they do not "belong" to us. Both things are important. If I have a thought, a feeling, or an opinion, I have to be able to be conscious of it. What I have to not do is confuse it with who I am. I am not the sum total of my thoughts, feelings, ideas or knowledge. These things are very transitory. I cannot put my self worth at stake whenever I have a thought or feeling. I can be wrong but it doesn't change or destroy me. If I can let go of ego involvement with things, then I can let go of a lot of fear and defensiveness. I no longer have to worry so much about being right.

What is Devotion?

The capacity for devotion is basic to lasting, healthy relationships. It is the ability to acknowledge and to treasure another person's essence as uniquely important and meaningful to you. Devotion is what allows us to go through serious challenges and to feel that we are still there for our partner, and our partner is still there for us. Devotion is a two-way proposition. Devotion to a partner who lacks the capacity for devotion does not provide a stable foundation. Before getting into recovery I lacked the capacity for devotion. I felt that putting so much of myself into a relationship with another person would be too risky. People who were looking for something solid in a partner undoubtedly sensed that I was unavailable in that way. Now I am devoted to my partner, but not because of this or that great attribute I see in them. Devotion is not blind, but it is about things I cannot name.

Appendix A

The Double Winner Promises of
Sex Addicts Anonymous

1. We will no longer see ourselves as merely predators or prey. Instead we will know ourselves to be integrated, whole, spiritual people, and we will let gratitude replace the view of ourselves as victims.

2. We will see that we are not so devastatingly complex that we cannot be understood. We will be able to recognize what we have in common with those we fear and resent.

3. We will experience our pain and anger but refuse to build shrines to our feelings. We will grow more respectful in the way we express our uncomfortable feelings.

4. We will forgive, and allow ourselves to be forgiven. We will make peace with our past, and with all parts of ourselves.

5. We will no longer confuse love with sex, emotional dependency or romantic intrigue.

6. We will feel at last at home in our own bones and discover precisely how beautiful we are.

7. We will be committed not merely to stopping our behaviors, but to finding a new way to live.

8. We will connect in honesty and integrity with our HP, our sponsor, our fellow addicts, our partners, our families and those around us. We will live transparent lives in which there are no secrets.

9. We will risk telling those truths about ourselves that cause us the most shame. At the same time, we will develop a healthy sense of caution in our relationships.

10. Our behavior will be in integrity with values that are rooted in our spirituality. We will find serenity and live in peace.

11. The fence between addict and co-addict will be transformed by empathy into a bridge of understanding with others.

12. Through trusting our Higher Power who transcends our addictions and co-addictions, we will learn to better trust ourselves and recognize trustworthy people.

Appendix B

The Promises of Recovering Couples Anonymous

If we are honest about our commitment and painstaking about working the Twelve Steps together, we will see these promises come true in our lives:

> We will be amazed at how soon our
>
> love will flourish,
>
> We will experience mutual forgiveness,
>
> We will trust each other,
>
> We will learn how to play and have fun together,
>
> We will be better partner, parents, workers,
>
> helpers, and friends.

No matter how close to brokenness we have come, we will be able to help others by sharing our experience, strength, and hope. Are these extravagant promises? We think not!

Just as our love for our partners has been imperfect, we may not always be adequately able to express to you the deep love and acceptance we feel for you. Keep coming back! The process of loving and communication grows in us and with each other one day at a time.

Bibliography

Adams, K. M. (2011) *Silently Seduced.* Deerfield Beach, FL: Health Communications, Inc.

Adams K.M. and Morgan, A.P. (2007) *When He's Married to Mom.* New York: Fireside Books.

Al-Anon Family Group Headquarters. (1990) *In All Our Affairs.* Virginia Beach, VA: Al-Anon Family Group Headquarters.

Alcoholics Anonymous World Services. (1976) *Alcoholics Anonymous.* New York: Alcoholics Anonymous World Services.

Beattie, Melody. (2000) *The Language of Letting Go.* Center City, MN: Hazelden Press.

Carnes, P.J. (1991) *Don't Call it Love: Recovery from Sexual Addiction.* New York: Bantam Books.

Carnes, P.J. (1994) *Out of the Shadows.* Center City, MN: Hazelden Press.

Carnes, P.J. (1997) *The Betrayal Bond: Breaking Free of Exploitive Relationships.* Deerfield Beach, FL: Health Communications Inc.

Carnes, P.J. (2009) *Recovery Zone, Vol.1.* Wickenburg, AZ: Gentle Path Press.

Carnes, P.J. (2010) *Facing the Shadow.* Carefree, AZ: Gentle Path Press.

Carnes, P. J., Laaser, D. and Laaser, M. (1999) *Open Hearts.* Wickenburg, AZ: Gentle Path Press.

Carnes, P.J. and Moriarity, J.M. (1997) *Sexual Anorexia: Overcoming Sexual Self-Hatred.* Center City, MN: Gentle Path Press.

CoDa Resource Publishing. (1995) *Co-Dependents Anonymous.* Dallas, Texas: CoDa Resource Publishing.

Flaws, B, & Wolfe, H. (1983) *Prince Wen Hui's Cook: Chinese Dietary Therapy.* Brookline MA: Paradigm Publications.

Forstater, M. (2001) *The Tao: Finding the Way of Balance and Harmony.* New York: Plume (An Imprint of the Penguin Group).

Gladwell, M. (2005) *Blink: The Power of Thinking without Thinking.* New York: Little, Brown and Company.

Gorski, T. T. (1993) *Addictive Relationships: Why Love Goes Wrong in Recovery.* Independence, Missouri: Herald House Independence Press.

Gottman, J.M.& Silver, N. (1999) *The Seven Principles for Making Marriage Work.* New York: Crown.

Harbach, C. (2011) *The Art of Fielding.* New York: Little, Brown and Company.

Hendrix, H. (1988) *Getting the Love You Want*. New York: Henry Holt and Company, LLC.

Katehakis, A. (2010) *Erotic Intelligence*. Deerfield Beach, FL: Health Communications, Inc.

Linehan, M. M. (1993) *Cognitive-Behavioral Treatment of the Borderline Personality Disorder*. New York: The Guilford Press.

Masterson, J. F. (1985) *The Real Self*. New York: Brunner/Mazel, Inc.

Mellody, P., Wells, A.W., & Miller, J.K. (1989) *Facing Codependence*. New York: Harper Collins Publishers, Inc.

Mellody, P. & Freundlich, L.S. (2004) *The Intimacy Factor*. New York: Harper Collins Publishers Inc.

Miller, S., Miller, P, Nunnally, E.W. & Wackman, D.B. (1991) *Talking & Listening Together*. Evergreen, CO: Interpersonal Communications Programs, Inc.

Nhat Hanh, T. (1975) *The Miracle of Mindfulness: An Introduction to the Practice of Meditation*. Boston, MA: Beacon Press.

O'Donohue, J. (2008) *To Bless the Space Between Us*. New York: Doubleday.

Olsen, D. H. Portner, J. & Lavee, Y. (2007) *Family Adaptability and Cohesion Evaluation Scale III*. in Fisher, J. & Corcoran, K. Measures for Clinical Practice and Research: A Sourcebook. New York: McGraw Hill.

Ruiz, M. A. (1997) *The Four Agreements*. San Rafael, CA: Amber Allen Publishing, Inc.

Saint-Exupery, A. (1968) *Wind, Sand and Stars*. New York: Harcourt Brace & Company.

Peter Pauper Press. Hanna, B., Buddha. (1957) *The Sayings of Buddha*. Mt. Vernon, N.Y.: Peter Pauper Press.

Schore, A.N. (1994) *Affect Regulation and the Origin of the Self*. Hillsdale, N.J. Lawrence Erlbaum Associates Publishers.

Tolle, E. (1999) *Practicing the Power of Now*. Novato, CA: New World Library.

Tolle, E. (2003) *Stillness Speaks*. Novato, CA: New World Library.

Van der Kolk, B.A., McFarlane, A.C., & Weisaeth, L. (1996) *Traumatic Stress*. New York: The Guilford Press.

Watts, A. (1989) *The Way of Zen*. New York: Vintage Books (An Imprint of Random House).

Whyte, D. (2002) *The Heart Aroused: Poetry and the Preservation of the Soul in Corporate America*. New York: Currency Books.

Made in the USA
Lexington, KY
01 November 2013